A Year of Cupcakes

Geraldine Kidwell

Schiffer Publishing Ltd®

4880 Lower Valley Road · Atglen, PA · 19310

Schiffer Books are available at special discounts for bulk purchases for sales promotions or premiums. Special editions, including personalized covers, corporate imprints, and excerpts can be created in large quantities for special needs. For more information contact the publisher:

Published by Schiffer Publishing Ltd.
4880 Lower Valley Road
Atglen, PA 19310
Phone: (610) 593-1777; Fax: (610) 593-2002
E-mail: Info@schifferbooks.com

For the largest selection of fine reference books on this and related subjects, please visit our web site at **www. schifferbooks.com**
We are always looking for people to write books on new and related subjects. If you have an idea for a book please contact us at the above address.

This book may be purchased from the publisher.
Include $5.00 for shipping.
Please try your bookstore first.
You may write for a free catalog.

In Europe, Schiffer books are distributed by
Bushwood Books
6 Marksbury Ave.
Kew Gardens
Surrey TW9 4JF England
Phone: 44 (0) 20 8392 8585; Fax: 44 (0) 20 8392 9876
E-mail: info@bushwoodbooks.co.uk
Website: www.bushwoodbooks.co.uk

Copyright © 2009 by Geraldine Kidwell
Library of Congress Control Number: 2009927265

Designed by RoS
Type set in Kaufmann BT/Zurich BT

ISBN: 978-0-7643-3198-5

Printed in China

Dedication

I would like to dedicate this "cupcake" book to all of my special sugar art friends and acquaintances who have been so generous in contributing their marvelous ideas and designs for my book endeavors. Each of these artists is extremely talented and sharing and I thank all of you for immediately offering to create designs when I asked. Your contributions have brought a broader scope of creations than I could have completed alone. I did not realize that so many new designs existed until you put on your thinking caps and started work. I thank each and every one of you. I treasure your friendship and admire your creativity.

Thanks to my husband Bill, our children, Bret, Gina and Lori, our grandchildren, Bretani, Collan, Hunter and Wesley and my mother Gladys. Each of these individuals contributes to my endeavors and to the person that I am. Thanks too go out to my photographers and dear friends, Sam and Elaine Stringer who have spent countless hours to assure that the included photographs are of perfect quality.

Acknowledgments

I would like to thank all of the wonderful decorators who contributed cupcake designs that were not used in this book. I wanted to use them but regretfully, the quality of a few of the photographs was not of the technical quality needed by the publisher. The largest number of these was from the girls participating in the Cincinnati, Ohio, cake show, and the largest project was from Millie Green of Indianapolis, Indiana, who created a magnificently full-size mermaid from dozens of cupcakes. Thank you for all your hard work.

Foreword

It is my pleasure to introduce and to express my opinion of Geraldine Kidwell for having been one of my best students in cake decoration. I am giving my opinion of her personality and her work with cakes. She has developed a wonderful talent in our profession, making big cakes, teaching and writing books with new ideas for lovely cakes. She is a distinguished member of our I.C.E.S. organization (International Cake Exploration Societe), serving as demonstrator, representative, and even president. My wish is for her to continue with her wonderful work in cake decorating in all aspects for the satisfaction and enjoyment of everyone that has the privilege of knowing her or being her friend.

Marithe de Alvarado
Instituto del Arte Mexicano del Azucar
Av. Cuauhtemoc 950
Col Narvarte
03020 Mexico D.F.

Contents

Introduction

Cupcakes have a long and tasty history. Through the years, two explanations have evolved as to how these little delicacies got their name. The first explanation is that the cake ingredients were originally meticulously weighed for accuracy. Around the late 1800s someone began to use cups to measure the ingredient amounts — a cup of sugar, a cup of milk, etc. — thus the name "cup" cake. Although this is a reasonable explanation, the measured cake was still standard size.

The other theory explains that large cakes baked in primitive ovens often dried out or burned in the time required to cook the center of the cake. To prevent this problem, little pottery cups were used so that the smaller amount of batter would cook quickly and evenly — thus a cup of cake or "cupcake." Soon the twelve cavity muffin tin was introduced on the market which was a perfect way to bake a dozen cupcakes in the more modern ovens.

The concept and popularity of the cupcake have grown through the years. Currently it has even reached celebrity status by appearing on the Food Network Cupcake Challenge and by occupying center stage at many weddings as the wedding cake focal point. The dictionary defines cupcake as a small individual cake. The contents of this book take that definition to a whole new dimension — from a single serving to individual cakes that are frosted together and appear to be one cake. Cupcakes are so popular at birthday parties, showers, work events, school parties, and weddings that a whole new market has opened up to support the popularity. Shaped cupcake pans for special holidays, cupcake fabric, cupcake gourmet accessories, decorative cupcake papers, plastic picks to be inserted into each cake and there are even laser cut cups to cover the paper cups.

1 *January*

CELEBRATING JANUARY

Baby New Year

Whether you celebrate the first day of January with Baby New Year or Father Time, another year has passed and a new one is beginning as everyone celebrates, makes resolutions, and plans for a brighter future. Whether you are celebrating with champagne or hot chocolate, I hope this New Year opens the door for all your dreams to come true.

Supplies
- 1 cupcake for each treat
- 2 tiny gum balls
- 1/4 pound of fondant
- Black food writer pen
- 1 inch x 2 inch piece wafer paper
- Food colors, pink, white, blue, black and brown
- Star tip # 18 – decorator bag
- Royal Frosting
- 1 piece of spaghetti

You can use gum paste or fondant to form your figures. I normally use fondant and add two teaspoons of tylose powder per pound to strengthen the paste. Mix the tylose into the paste and allow it to cure overnight in a sealable plastic bag before you use it.

Color a golf ball-size piece of fondant with a light pink or other coloring appropriate for your ethnic preference, until you get the desired flesh color for a baby. Form four balls of the pink. One ball should be the same size as one of the tiny gum balls and three balls should be twice the size of the gum ball. Keep the balls covered in a plastic bag or with plastic wrap to prevent them from drying.

To form the torso, roll one of the larger balls until it is perfectly smooth. Hold the ball in the palm of your hand and press a gum ball into the paste until you can feel it firmly against your palm. Work the paste up over the ball. Continue to work the paste upward to form the torso into a pear shape and smooth the body with your fingertips. Press a small piece of spaghetti into the neck of the torso to support the head. Push a small ball tool or the rounded end of a small paintbrush into the tummy area and slightly pull down to form the navel. On the back of the baby use a small skewer or paintbrush handle to press and form a crease to mark the two sides of the little baby bottom.

To form the head, roll the second large ball of paste until smooth. Repeat the process that used to incorporate a gum ball into the torso. Cover the ball, working the excess paste to the neck where it can be trimmed. Flatten the area of the head where the eyes will be and form a bulge on each side of the face for puffy cheeks. Roll a tiny ball and secure it for the nose. Shape the mouth exactly the same as you did for the naval by inserting a rounded object and pulling it slightly down and out.

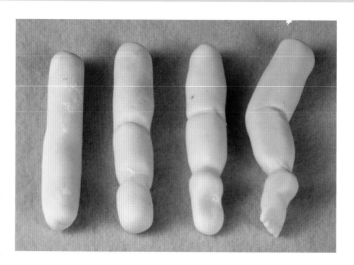

Steps to form legs/feet

Divide the third large ball into two equal parts for form two legs. Cover one half to prevent drying and roll the other half into a very smooth ball. Roll the ball into a log shape. Lightly score the log in the middle to mark the knee. Divide the lower half of the log shape in half again and mark lightly for the ankle. Thin this mark between your thumb and forefinger to form the ankle. Flatten the foot and shape. Form the heel, cut the toes, and bend the knee. Flatten the hip area to attach the leg to the body with royal frosting. Repeat this process for the second leg being careful to have a right and left foot. You will need to decide at this point how you will position your legs on the finished figurine and prop them to dry in that position.

The arms are formed by dividing the small ball of fondant into two halves. Repeat the process exactly as described for the legs. Thin the wrist and flatten hand. Cut a "V" shape from the hand to form the thumb. Cut the fingers with small manicure scissors and roll each slightly to thin and curve it to shape. Flatten the shoulder area of the arm so it will fit. Repeat the process for the second arm, being careful to have a right and a left hand. Prop each in the correct position to dry on tissues.

The facial features of your character will give it personality. If you feel you need practice, you can experiment on a scrap piece of fondant or waxed paper. Paint the eye area with bright white food color. Allow it to dry and paint the iris with either blue or brown food color. After these two steps have dried, add a black pupil to each eye. Add two or three eye lashes with a very tiny brush and black food color.

The hair is formed with light brown fondant. Lay a small, gum ball-size piece of brown fondant in the palm of your hand and push the gum ball into the paste to form a cup shape. Remove the gum ball and place the cup over the head of the baby. Secure the hair with a small amount of royal frosting. Form hair lines with a modeling tool or the dull side of a table knife. Press the tool into the soft paste and pull down to blend the hair onto the neck and face.

To assemble the figurine, attach the head, secure it with royal frosting, and allow it to dry. The arms can also be attached with royal frosting but it is necessary to prop them in place until the drying process is complete.

Position the legs on either side of the body and attach with royal frosting. Cut a triangle of light blue fondant for the diaper. Set the baby on top of the diaper. Pull the front point of the triangle up between the baby's legs. Twist the sides and bring them to the front over the top of the point. Trim the sides if necessary and fold the front point down over the twisted sides. Allow the back of the diaper to droop to show the crack in the baby bottom.

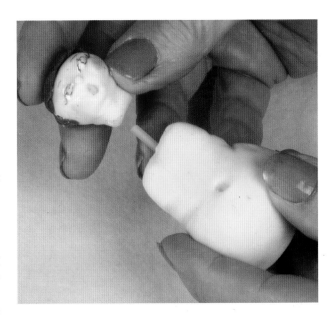

Adding hair & attaching head

To form the banner, roll and cut a strip of white fondant that is 1/2 inch wide x 9 inches long. Drape the banner around the shoulders and neck of the baby while the past is still soft. When the paste dries, use a black, food-safe pen to inscribe the year and message.

The top hat is made from a small, pea-size ball of black fondant. Roll a small piece very thin and cut a round circle with the large end of a decorator tip to form the brim. Roll and elongate the remainder piece of black and form into the top of the hat. Dampen slightly to attach the two pieces, then place it on the head of the baby.

Roll a small pea-size piece of white fondant and shape into a small cone shape. Insert a small paint brush handle into the larger end of the horn and create an opening for the horn. Allow to dry and paint gold. Attach in the baby's mouth with a touch of royal frosting.

Cut a 1 inch wide x 2 inch long piece of wafer paper into a triangle flag. Fold the large end around a piece of spaghetti and attach with royal. Write the year on the flag with a black, food-safe pen. Place the flag in the baby's hand and attach with royal frosting.

Frost a standard-size cupcake with a #18 decorator tip and a swirling motion. Set the baby on the soft frosting and sprinkle generously with sugar confetti. These little babies can be made well in advance and stored until the last minute to save time during the hectic holiday season.

Making banner

Time to Celebrate

The clock strikes twelve on New Years Eve and it's time to celebrate a brand new year.

Supplies
- 1 cupcake for each treat
- Food markers, black and pink
- Tiny candies
- Royal frosting
- 1 decorator bag and # 4 or 5 writing tip
- Waxed paper

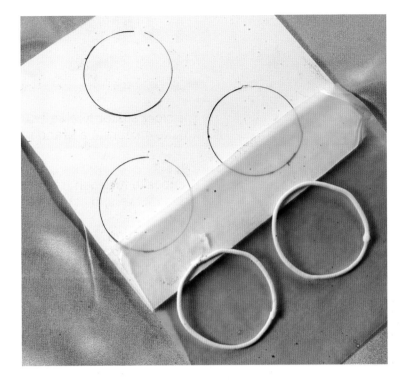

Trace patterns

Trace round patterns, approximately 3 inches in diameter, onto a piece of cardboard. Cover the pattern with a square of waxed paper and slightly attach it to prevent sliding. Outline the circle with firm consistency royal frosting and allow the line to dry.

Thin additional royal frosting until it will run freely from a spoon. Place it in a decorator bag and flood the inside of the circle. Set aside to dry — at least 24 hours and possibly more depending on your humidity.

Draw the eyes and mouth with a black, food-safe marker. Add the numbers 12, 3, 6, and 9 and fill in the additional number spots with tiny candies. Add little fondant clock hands pointing to midnight.

Frost the cupcake and add the plaque while the frosting is damp. The plaques can be made well in advance and stored.

Flood the circle

Draw facial features

Mr. Snowman

In my geographic location, January brings frigid temperatures and drifting snow. We have a lot of weather-related school closing, so it is a perfect time for the kids to build snowmen. These eatable ones will just add to the fun, especially when served with a steaming cup of hot chocolate.

Supplies
- 2 regular size cupcakes
- 1 mini cupcake
- Golf ball-size red fondant
- 2 stick pretzels or brown fondant
- 1 piece spaghetti
- Small candies or black fondant for eyes and buttons
- White butter cream

Bake and cool the cupcakes. Remove the paper holders and let them air dry for 1 to 2 hours. Use kitchen shears to round the edges of the two cupcakes that will be on top. Stack the cupcakes, placing the mini cupcake on top for the head. Use a spot of frosting between the layers and insert a piece of heavy spaghetti into the head and thru all of the cupcakes for added support.

Completely frost the cupcakes. Use a paper towel to smooth and round the three balls. Set the snowman aside to firm while you make the accent pieces.

Secure cup cakes with spaghetti

To form the scarf, roll a long, narrow strip of red fondant. Use a pizza cutter to trim the scarf approximately 1/2 inch wide x 9 inches long. Make small cuts on each end for the fringe. Wrap the scarf around the neck, twist it in front, and allow the ends to drape down the side.

To create the hat, roll a piece of red fondant and cut a 4 inch triangle. Dampen one edge and wrap the triangle around the pointed end of a small paper drinking cup to shape. Bend the point to the side and fold up the lower edge. Place the cap on the snowman's head and add a small ball of red for the pom-pom.

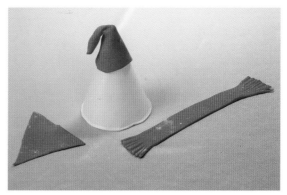

Forming the scarf and shaping the hat

Roll small black balls of fondant, or use tiny black candies, and place them for the eyes and buttons. Roll a tiny, pointed orange fondant carrot shape for the nose and place in the center of the face.

The arms can be pretzel sticks or brown fondant that is rolled around short pieces of spaghetti. Push into the center cupcake on either side of the body and attach a flat, red mitten to each arm.

Place the completed snow man on a tray and add frosting for snow. Sprinkle the snow generously with sanding sugar or glitter.

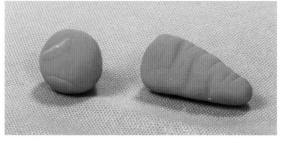

Carrot shape nose

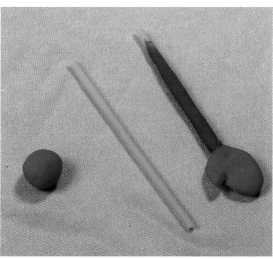

Pretzel arms

January Guest Contributors

Design: Dathern Moon
Huntsville, Alabama
Photo: Steve Cassidy
Huntsville, Alabama

This handmade, artistically sculpted snowman is designed using white modeling chocolate. Each piece is made separately. Dathern prefers to use white chocolate because it has long lasting qualities that the designer can not get from other ingredients. The snowman is sitting on top of a white chocolate, 2 inch diameter tier.

Design by Dathern Moon, Huntsville, AL
Photo by Steve Cassidy, Huntsville, AL

Design: Maria Regina Padel Rodrigues
Rio de Janeiro, Brazil
Photo: Christopher Kubota
Rio de Janeiro, Brazil

The delicate little flowers on this lovely Brazialian creation are sure to delight any crowd. It is smooth frosted then adorned with tiny gum paste flowers and leaves.

Design by Regina Rodriguez, Rio de Janeiro, Brazil, Photo by Christopher Kubota, Rio de Janeiro, Brazil

Design & photos: Christine Clark
Cincinnati, Ohio

This delightful hot chocolate cupcake mug design is perfect for the cold days of winner. It is so realistic that you can almost see it steaming.

Hot Chocolate mug design and photo courtesy of Christine Clark, Cincinnati, OH

Design & photos: Carol Webb
　Albany, Oregon

　Carol's mold # 533 is used for the wrap on these cupcakes. Dust the mold with cornstarch and press fondant into it. Trim off any excess with a pallet knife. Turn the mold upside down onto a work area to fall out to prevent stretching. This can be dried around a short tapered glass so the cupcake will set into it. You can also apply the basket directly to the cupcake with the use of butter cream. The roses are made from mold #749 and the leaves molded from NY Miami Sweets Fantasy leaf set.

Design and Photos courtesy of Carol Webb, Albany, OR

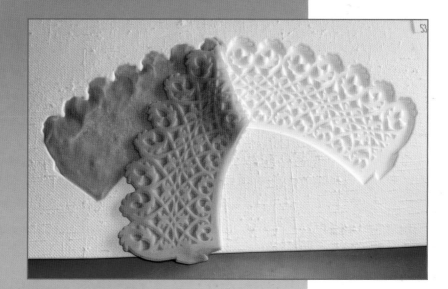

2 *February*
OCCASIONS

The year is underway and with February comes many occasions that we continue to celebrate including Marti Gras, Presidents Day and a very special day for lovers, Valentine's Day.

Mardi Gras

Mardi Gras is a traditional holiday celebrated in many southern states. The most famous celebration takes place in the French Quarters of New Orleans, Louisiana. The holiday features numerous masquerade balls where people dress in costumes and the famous Mardi Gras masks.

Supplies
- 1 standard cupcake
- 1 mini cupcake
- Silicone Plastique (MakeYourOwn-Molds.com)
- Small face to mold
- Bead maker
- AmeriColors – white, teal, red, black, purple
- Brushes

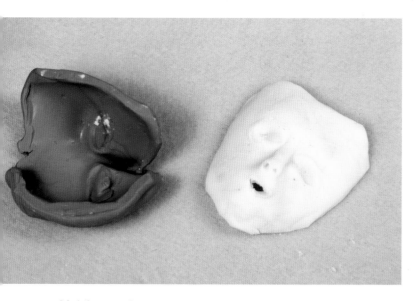

Molding mask

If you do not have a small face mold then you can easily create one by using a small face and Silicone Plastique to make your own original mold. Plastique has the consistency of clay. It comes in a jar of blue and a jar of white silicone. Combine equal parts of the two substances and work them together until the two are uniform in color and incorporated as one. Rub a small amount of the mixture into the details of your face, creating an initial thin layer. Apply a second layer, at least one quarter inch thick, completely covering the object's surface. To bond correctly, layers of Plastique must be applied before the previous layer has fully cured. After mixing the Plastique has a workable consistency for about 20-30 minutes. Allow the mold to dry several hours before removing the face.

Press soft gum paste or fondant into the facial mold to form the mask. Press firmly into all of the facial cavities and gently remove. Place on a curved surface to dry overnight.

Paint the entire mask with white liquid AmeriColor food coloring. Allow the surface to dry before adding details as shown. Set aside to dry.

Frost one standard and one mini cupcake with butter cream or fondant. Place the mini cupcake on top of the standard size toward the back. The stacked cakes provide a stand for the mask so that it can be elevated rather than flat. Use a small amount of frosting to secure the mask tilted against the mini cake.

Roll a long, thin log of colored fondant or gum paste. Insert the paste into the larger cavity of the bead maker and work thoroughly into the grooves. Trim off any excess. Gently bend the mold and remove the beads. Arrange two or three strands of various color beads around the mask and over the top of the cupcakes allowing them to drape to the table surface.

Painting mask

Be My Valentine

If there is a special someone in your life, then Valentine's Day is an important day for you. Everyone young or old, single or married wants to be appreciated and to know that they are remembered by their Valentine on this special day for lovers.

Supplies
- 8 standard size cupcakes
- Red buttercream frosting
- 1/2 pound white fondant
- 2 pieces heavy spaghetti
- Silicone bead maker
- 1 package Wilton sugar hearts
- 1 heart shaped cake board
- Small scissors

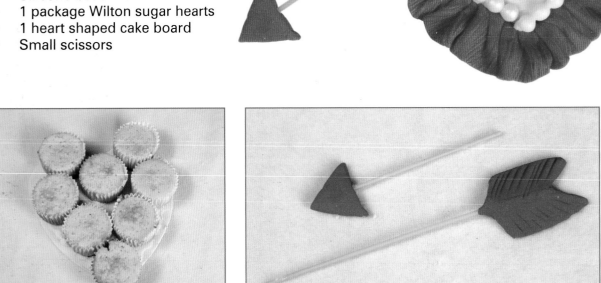

Arrange cup cakes on heart   Form arrow

Cut a cake board or a piece of foam core board to a heart shape that will hold the 8 cupcakes. Arrange the cupcakes on the board as pictured and attach with a small amount of frosting. Frost the tops of the arrangement of cupcakes with red frosting as one cake.

Roll a long strip of white fondant to a thin consistency and cut a 1 to 1-1/2 inch wide strip. Pleat the strip to form a ruffle and attach around the edge of the heart.

Cut a 1 inch wide x 2 inch long strip of fondant and insert a piece of heavy spaghetti into the center of the piece. With small scissors, fringe each side to resemble a feather. On a second piece of spaghetti form a trianglur piece of fondant for the point of the arrow.

Powder the cavity of the large pearl bead maker with pearl luster. Press a long strip of fondant into the cavity. Remove the strand of pearls and use it to border the edge of the ruffle around the heard. Continue making strands until you have enough to circle the heart.

Remove 3 of the sugar hearts from the card and place on the cake. Insert the feather piece of the arrow into the top of the cake at an angle. Insert the pointed piece into the side so that it looks like the arrow is one long piece going through the heart. You can inscribe a message or just let your valentine know that he/she has been hit with cupid's arrow.

Something for My Beau

If you want something a little less feminine for the male valentine in your life, these tuxedo strawberries are sure to express your love

Supplies
- standard size cupcakes
- red or white frosting
- white chocolate coating
- milk chocolate coating
- Large perfect strawberries
- Small red sugar hearts (Wilton)

Dip strawberries in chocolate

Add buttons and bow tie

Bake several standard size cupcakes and frost with red or white icing. Select some large, perfect strawberries. Rinse and dry them thoroughly on a paper towel. Leave the green top on the strawberries.

Melt some white chocolate in one container and milk chocolate in a second container. It is best if the container has a smaller diameter so the chocolate will be deeper in the container. Hold the green stem and submerge the strawberry in white chocolate, leaving a small circle of the red fruit around the base of the cap. Allow the white to set up. To speed the process you can set the fruit in the refrigerator or freezer for a few minutes.

Hold the strawberry at an angle and dip one side of the berry into milk chocolate. Set the berry aside to dry again. When the chocolate is set, dip the opposite side of the berry into the milk chocolate as pictured.

Using a pointed object such as a toothpick or skewer, dip it into the chocolate and make tiny dots on the front of the "shirt" for buttons. Use a little more chocolate to create the bow tie. When the chocolate has cooled and is firm, place a completed strawberry on each cupcake. To add a special touch for valentines, add a small sugar heart to each tuxedo cupcake.

Washington's Birthday

"I can not tell a lie. I cut down the cherry tree." Famous words from George Washington. These little logs are the perfect way to bring history alive and to celebrate George Washington's birthday.

Supplies
- 3 mini cupcakes
- Chocolate frosting
- Tip # 20
- 1 decorator bag
- 3 or 4 maraschino cherries with stems

Bake and cool mini cupcakes. Remove the cupcake papers. Slightly trim and flatten one side of each cupcake so it will lie flat. Lay them on their sides and add frosting between each cupcake to form a little log.

Insert a #20 decorator tip into a decorating bag and fill the bag with chocolate frosting. Use long horizontal strokes to cover the log. Use a small offset spatula or a fork to rough the "log" to resemble tree bark.

To form the hatchet handle, cut a narrow strip of fondant approximately 2-1/2 inches long x 3/4 inch wide making it wider at one end. Cut a small triangle piece for the ax head. Attach the two pieces and allow them to dry. Paint the ax head silver and the handle brown. Add tiny dark brown or black lines to the handle to resemble wood grain.

Prop the handle into the log and allow to dry. Add two or three long stem maraschino cherries before serving.

Shaping the log

Design: Alexandra Pappas
Nashville, Tennessee

A perfect rose for a perfect Valentine. This beautiful gum paste rose is formed from gum paste thinly rolled then cut with a rose leaf cutter. The petals are attached with gum glue while the paste is still soft and pliable. Prop the outside petals until dry then place on a standard size frosted cupcake.

Design: Susan Zugehoer
Hebron Kentucky

Interlocked hearts are cut from thin red gum paste and placed on the top of the cupcake. Personalize each with a message inscribed with a #1 decorator tip and black icing or a food-safe marker can be used on the heart if it has dried thoroughly. Add a red and white border around the edge of the top.

Below:
Design: Steven Stellingwerf
Sioux Falls, South Dakota

To create this lovely little treat, Steve covered the cupcake with butter cream then with fondant which he rolled and cut the height of the cupcake side. He rolled an embossed rolling pin over more fondant and used a round cookie cutter to cut a circle the same size as the top of the cupcake. He brushed it with pearl luster dust and placed it on top of the little cake. The bottom border was royal icing piped with a #362 then #2 pink dots were added. The top border was piped using a #3 tip. The flowers and leaves were hand molded using teardrop and circle shapes. The designs were impressed using an icing spatula and quilting wheel and dusted with luster dust. The desert was then displayed on a small milk glass pedestal stand.

Right:
Design & photo: Rosa Viacava de Ortega
Lima, Peru

Cover a 2 inch cupcake with blue fondant. Work white gum paste to make the special Bianca lace with tiny eyelets (BOK-001) and glue at the base of the cupcake. Prepare five pieces of white Cinderella lace (BOK-002) and glue diagonally around the cake. Cut the hummingbird (0R07-013) in white gum paste and wire it, dry and paint it with luster dust. Insert the wire of the hummingbird into the cupcake. Supplies available at www.RosasDesigns.com

Design & photo: Carol Webb
Albany, Oregon

The covering for this lovely fondant covered cupcake was molded in the cavity of ELI mold # 532. You can reduce the size by using a scalloped edge cookie cutter of the appropriate size. Flowers were made from NY Miami Sweets 5 petal cutter set. They were dried in a CK South mold # 43-9003 and leaves were made from ELI mold #749.

Design: Claudette Tidwell
Nashville, Tennessee

Two red marzipan hearts adorn the top of this butter cream cupcake for that special Valentine's party.

3 March
CELEBRATING ST. PATRICK'S DAY

March is strongly colored with our Irish heritage. St. Patrick's Day highlights a lucky month full of leprechauns, shamrocks and a pot of gold at the end of the rainbow.

Over the Rainbow

The pot of gold at the end of the rainbow is a sought after treasure that only escapes detection through the trickery and evasiveness of the leprechaun.

Supplies
- 2 dozen standard size cupcakes
- Fondant – red, orange, yellow, blue, indigo, lavender and black
- Gold chocolate coins
- Black, green and white butter cream

Arrange 21 to 22 cupcakes in a semi circle around the edge of a 16 inch cake board leaving the papers intact. Frost the tops as one cake with white butter cream. Roll a long log of each color and roll together to blend the colors in one strip. Lay the strip over the arch of cupcakes and mold and contour it to the arch shape.

Remove the paper from two cupcakes and frost the larger top ends together so the black pot is larger in the middle and narrow at the top and bottom. Cut a narrow black fondant strip approximately 1/3 inch wide. Form the strip into a ring and add it to the top of the pot. Slightly flare out the top edge of the rim.

Frost the lower half of the board with green butter cream for grass and position the black pot in the lower center of the arch. Generously fill the pot and sprinkle the base of the rainbow with gold covered chocolate coins.

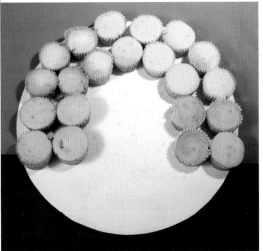

Arrange cup cakes in a semi circle

Leprechaun Luck

This elusive little fellow is sure to be a hit at every St. Patrick's Day event. Try to eat him quickly before he disappears.

Supplies
- 2 standard size cupcakes
- 1 sucker
- Tips #14, 12, and 3
- Black food safe pen
- Fondant, green, flesh pink and black
- Gold coins
- Brown royal frosting
- Butter cream frosting

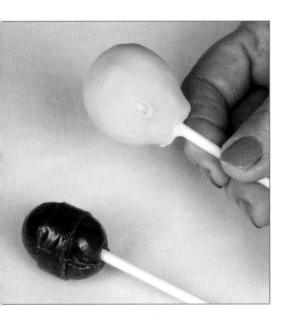

Form leprechaun head

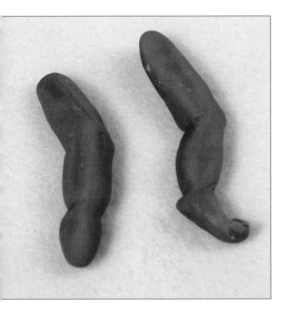

Form legs

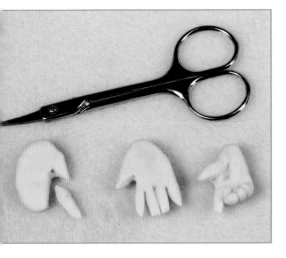

Shape hands

To form the head, cover the sucker with flesh color fondant. Smooth and work any excess to the neck of the sucker stick area and trim.

Paint eyes on the head by forming two black oval spots with a food safe pen. Form the mouth by inserting a small ball tool into the soft paste and pull down. The nose is a tiny ball of matching fondant.

Cut a circle for the hat brim from green paste by using the open end of a large decorator tip. Brush a little gum glue on top of the head and attach the brim to the head. Contour the brim to the shape of the head and bend it up on one side. Shape an additional ball of paste for the crown of the hat as pictured and attach it to the brim.

Remove the paper cups from two standard cupcakes and stack them together with butter cream. Frost the ensemble. Cover the body with green fondant or rolled butter cream.

Insert the sucker head into the cupcake ensemble. If it does not seat firmly, lift it up and cut an inch from the end of the stick so it will fit snugly against the body area.

Use a #14 star tip and green butter cream to pipe down the front and around the hem of the jacket. Pipe a brown mustache, hair and beard with butter cream or royal and a #3 writing tip. Swirl the tube in a slight circular motion to form curly hair and beard. Use a #12 writing tip to pipe green arms for the body. Beginning at the neck edge of the shoulder, pipe nearly to the waist, then bend the arm in a right angle toward the center front.

Form a ball of green fondant and divide into two equal parts to form the legs. Cover one half to prevent it from drying and roll a very smooth ball with the other half. Roll the ball into a log shape. Visually divide the log in half and score lightly with the dull side of a table knife. This mark will later be the back of the knee.

Visually divide the lower half of the log shape in half again and mark it for the ankle. Thin this mark between your thumb and forefinger to form the ankle.

Flatten the foot area and shape. Form the heel and pull the toe of the shoe to a point and roll the end around a short skewer to resemble a pixie shoe. Flatten the hip area and attach to the leprechaun. Repeat the process for the second leg.

Roll a large marble-size piece of flesh colored paste and divide into half for two hands. Flatten one ball for the hand and thin and narrow it at the wrist area. Cut a "V" shape from the hand to form the thumb. Cut the fingers with small manicure scissors and roll the fingers slightly to thin and curve them to shape. Repeat the process for the second hand, being careful to have a right and a left hand. Insert the hands into the sleeves and run a cuff of light green with the #14 tip at the sleeve and hand connection. Pipe an additional cuff around the hem line of the legs.

Sprinkle a few chocolate-covered gold coins around the cake plate.

Lucky Shamrock

A shamrock or four leaf clover is so simple to reproduce in cupcake that anyone can create a centerpiece that will receive rave reviews. Three or four heart cupcakes are used for a shamrock or for a lucky four leaf clover.

Supplies
- 3 or 4 small heart-shaped cupcakes
- Green butter cream
- Apple green sprinkling sugar
- Small ball green fondant
- Gold foil chocolate covered coins

Bake and cool the heart-shaped cupcakes. Frost each with green butter cream frosting and smooth the frosting with a pattern-less paper towel. Arrange three hearts for a shamrock or four for a lucky clover.

Form a log shape stem of green fondant that is narrow at the top and wider at the base. Insert the stem into position between two of the hearts. Sprinkle the finished cake generously with apple green sprinkling sugar.

Frost with green butter cream

Form a log shape stem

Raspberry Swirl Deserts

Supplies
- 1 white cake mix
- 1 package frozen raspberries
- 7 minute frosting
- Whipped cream

Place one package frozen raspberries, 1 cup sugar and 2 cups water in a saucepan. Bring the mixture to a boil and simmer five minutes. Mix 2 tablespoons cornstarch in 1/4 cup cold water and mix until it is dissolved. Stir the corn starch into the hot mixture and stir to thicken. Remove it from the heat and run the mix through a sieve to remove the seeds. You will have a thick, smooth, raspberry sauce. Swirl a tablespoon of the raspberry sauce into the cupcake batter, then bake.

Remove the paper and place a cupcake into a desert dish. Cover it with 7 minute frosting and top with whipped cream. Drizzle more of the raspberry sauce over the top and garnish with a few whole red raspberries.

Place cup cake in desert glass

Cover with 7 minute frosting

Garnish with whipped cream and raspberries

Design courtesy Regina Rodriguez, Rio
de Janeiro, Brazil, Photo by Christopher
Kubota, Rio de Janeiro, Brazil

Above:
Design: Regina Rodriguez
   Rio de Janeiro, Brazil
Photo: Christopher Kubota
   Rio de Janeiro, Brazil

   These beautiful cupcakes from Brazil are covered in colored fondant, then adorned with clusters
of hand-molded gum paste hydrangeas in hues of
blue, violet, and pink that would be gorgeous for
any occasion.

Right:
Design: Dathern Moon
   Huntsville, Alabama,
Photo: Steve Cassidy
   Huntsville, Alabama

   The balloons are brightly colored to blend with
the party theme using colored white modeling
chocolate. The melted white chocolate was poured
into the cupcake liner. The balloon stems were
inserted into the chocolate just before it hardened.
The packages were made from fondant and placed
on top of the cupcake.

Design and photo courtesy of Mariella Ortega
Viacava, Pembroke Pines, FL

Design and photo courtesy of Mirta
Carvajal de Alvarado, Lima, Peru

Above:
Design & photo: Mirta Carvajal de Alvarado
Lima, Peru

Sugar paste cymbidium orchids look so real
that they appear to be growing on the little white
cupcake. Blossoms are hand-molded from gum
paste and brushed with realistic color.

Left:
Design & photo: Mariella Ortega Viacava
Pembroke Pines, Florida

Model the face from a 1-1/2 inch ball of flesh
tone fondant. Attach a red ball for the nose. Open
the mouth with a stick and color with red. Roll and
cut little red circles for the cheeks and paint the
eyes. Roll yellow fondant and place on a zig-zag
ruler (BOK-003) to cut the thin hair, gluing to form
heavier areas. Form the hat from a 2 inch cone
of fondant and use almendra flowers (BOK-004
Rosa's Designs).

Roll a rounded blue fondant cone that is 3
inches, then mark legs and add details. The arms
are two logs of light yellow fondant that are 1-1/2
inches long. Bend each at the middle and add details with the zig-zag ruler in blue and bright yellow.
Form the black fondant shoes from a small 1-1/2
inch cone and add details with the zig-zag ruler.

Design & photo: Earlene Moore
Lubbock, TX

Design and photo courtesy of
Earlene Moore, Lubbock, TX

The coin molds for this "Bag of Coins" are made from silicone plastique. Mold the coins well in advance before you need them. The detail is not visible until you paint them. The cupcakes are baked in the extra-large tins and trimmed to give a more rounded shape. Roll colored fondant as thin as you can handle it on a textured mat. Pipe butter cream icing over the cupcake and bring fondant up to surround the entire cupcake, leaving a small opening at the top for the coins. Airbrush the bag lightly to give an appearance of used leather. Use the Sugarcraft gun and chocolate fondant to extrude the lacing pieces that are inserted around the top of the bag. Place coins on top of the bags and real coins can be used on the table around the cupcakes.

Design & photo: Christine Clark
Cincinnati, Ohio

This illusive little leprechaun is hand molded and sits nestled in a pot of gold, chocolate covered coins.

4 *April*
SIGNS OF SPRING

We know that spring is just around the corner when we see shelves of Easter bunnies, baby chicks and ducklings abounding in the stores to the children's delight. So much excitement is associated with these little characters that it seems appropriate to incorporate each into April cupcakes.

Easter Bunny

This fluffy little bunny is so easy to create that the kids can assist for their school party or other special events.

Supplies
* 1/2 cup white royal frosting
* 1/2 cupcake size ball pan
* Tiny paint brush and food safe pens
* White butter cream frosting
* Coconut
* 1 large marshmallow
* Bunny head pattern
* Small scissors
  * #3 decorator tip
* Decorator bag

Outline and flood the head with royal frosting

In advance, place the bunny head pattern under a sheet of waxed paper. Secure the paper to prevent it from slipping. Put a small amount of royal frosting into a decorator bag using a #3 writing tip. Draw an outline around the outside of the pattern with the royal. Allow the outline to dry for a few minutes until it sets up. Continue to outline all the additional heads that you plan to make.

Add just a few drops of water to the royal until it will run smoothly from the tip of the spoon and blend into the bowl. Place some of the frosting into the decorator bag and flood the area inside the dried outline. Allow the heads to dry overnight before adding the facial features with a fine line brush and food color or food safe marker pens. Gently peel the waxed paper from the heads.

Bake cupcakes that are a half-ball shape. Frost a cooled cake with butter cream and roll the damp frosting in a bowl of coconut. Omit the coconut from a small area on front of the body and attach the pre-formed head with a little additional frosting.

Using kitchen scissors, trim the square areas from both ends of the marshmallow. Cut a diagonal slice across one end of the marshmallow. Use the large piece for the bunny tail. Divide the small slice in half. Discard one half and divide the second half to form two feet. Make small cuts for the toes and attach them in place.

Roll in coconut

Hatching Chick

As the grass begins to turn green and trees begin to bud, new life is apparent everywhere as the baby chick breaks through his shell and views the world around him.

Supplies
- 2 egg-shaped cup-cake halves
- White butter cream or fondant
- A small brush & black food color or a black food pen
- 1 yellow gum ball
- 1 pea size ball of orange fondant

Join two egg halves together and frost in white

Place head on egg and add beak

Draw black cracks in egg

Bake and cool the two egg shape cupcakes. Trim the tops so that they will be flat and fit together tightly. Add frosting between the halves and stick them together. Cut a small round hole in the top cake for the chick to set. Frost the entire egg in white butter cream or fondant and smooth.

Insert the yellow gum ball into the top hole and attach it with a little frosting. Add two black dots for the eye. To form the beak, roll a tiny log of orange fondant and flatten it. Point the little log at each end and fold it in half. Attach the beak to the mouth area of the chick.

If the egg is frosted in butter cream, allow the frosting to crust before painting the black cracks around the chick. Should the egg be frosted in fondant you can use a black food safe marker for the cracks.

The grass around this little chick is especially appealing because it is eatable of shredded wafer paper, sprinkled with jelly beans.

Baby Duckling

Fuzzy little baby ducks swimming on a pool of blue are sure to delight any crowd of youngsters or even adults for your special spring gathering.

Supplies
- Two egg-shaped cupcake halves
- Yellow frosting
- 1 sucker or Tootsie Pop
- A golf ball-size piece of yellow fondant
- A small piece or orange and black fondant
- Small scissors

Trim two egg halves and frost them together with butter cream. The entire duck body can be covered with either yellow butter cream or fondant.

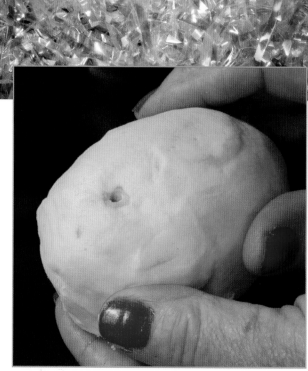

Frost 2 egg halves together

Frost duck body

Cover a sucker in yellow fondant for the duck's head

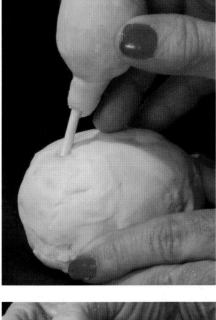

Insert head into body

Form and attach beak

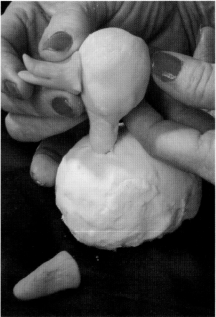

Roll a walnut-size piece of yellow fondant until it is smooth. Place the ball in the palm of your hand and firmly insert the sucker into the fondant. Smooth and work the paste to the base of the sucker. Work the paste around the stick to form a neck that is 1/2 to 1 inch in diameter. Cut an inch from the length of the stick and insert the head into the top of the cupcake body.

Form a log from a marble-size ball of orange fondant for the beak. Flatten and shape one end to fit on the duck head. Round and point the beak. Cut the end slightly and shape. Attach the beak to the head with a little frosting. Shape two small balls of black fondant. Flatten and attach each for eyes.

Roll a thin piece of yellow fondant. Use the enclosed patterns to cut two wings and a tail. Use small scissors to cut feathers. Attach the wings to either side of the duck body and position the tail at the upper back.

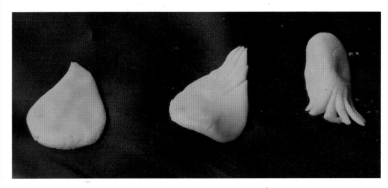

Cut wings and tail feathers and add to the body.

**Design & photo
by Barbara Green**
  Winchester,
Kentucky

   The panorama
egg is also
molded from
sugar. After the
two egg halves
are attached,
Barbara places
them in a cup
or small glass to
dry in an upright
position. The
cupcake is frosted
in pink and white
basket weave
with accents of
piped grass and
drop flowers. Tiny
sugar figurines
adorn the inside of
the egg to create a
scene.

Design: Irene Leach
Miami, Florida

Baby blocks and hand molded animals surround this fondant covered cupcake. The border is designed with a baby design impression roller available from Cuqui's Designs.

Design: Irene Leach
Miami, Florida

The adorable little hand molded baby graces the top of a fondant covered cupcake. The baby design fondant ribbon around the base is impressed with an impression roller available from Cuqui's Designs.

Design: Kathy Scott
Abbeville, South Carolina

These petite little Tiffany®-like boxes are covered with a thin coating of white chocolate in a special mold. Fondant is pressed into a design mold to form the artistic lid for each little cake box. Complete kits are available from Sweet Express.

Design: Leigh Sipe
Harrodsburg, Kentucky

This realistic little armadillo is sure to delight everyone. The body is formed with one mini loaf cake topped with one small egg-shaped cupcake to round the body. Form the head, tail, feet and cover the entire body with gray fondant.

Design & photo: Earlene Moore
Lubbock, Texas

These spring butterflies and daisies are perfect for any spring festival. Place wafer paper over a butterfly pattern and trace with a black felt tip fine point pen or food marker. Turn the paper over and trace the opposite side. Color the top sides of your butterfly wings using Q-tips® and colored chalk. Begin with the lightest shades of color and work to the darker. Earlene prefers to use the rough side for the tops of the wings. If the humidity is high, the wings will curl up slightly when the rough side is up.

Let dry completely and turn over to color the backside. Cut out the butterfly with an X-acto® knife (on cardboard) leaving the center connecting the wings. Fold gently in the center of the butterfly. Fold stiff paper and wax paper into a loose accordion shape. Butterflies will be placed in the bottom of the folds for the first drying and over the top fold for the second drying stage. With royal icing make a body with a #2 or #3 tip. Insert antennas into the head. You can use black stamens, black licorice, or black rice paper.

The daisy is molded from a First Impression Mold #FL204 Daisy. The center was brushed with thinned piping gel and then a mixture of cornmeal, yellow sugar and gelatin is sprinkled over the piping gel to give a realistic center. Green butter cream is used to add a few accent piped leaves.

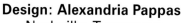

Design: Alexandria Pappas
Nashville, Tennessee

Seven mini cupcakes form this spring flower. The center of the flower is frosted with yellow using a grass tip. Six white (or color of your choice) frosted mini cupcakes are arranged around the center. Two green gum drop leaves are attached to the candy stem. Two wafer paper butterflies have landed for a taste of the sweet nectar.

Design & photo: Barbara Green
Winchester, Kentucky

The broken egg shell is molded of sugar. The mixture is 1 cup granulated sugar mixed with 1-1/2 teaspoons water. Mix well and pack in half a plastic egg and turn out to dry. Test after one hour. If the shell has dried 1/4 inch deep, carefully scrap out the moist sugar and let dry again. Barbara breaks the edges of the egg to resemble a cracked egg. Pipe the chicken with a #10 decorator tip and yellow frosting. Pull to the front to form a beak. Pipe #6 wings on each side. Paint the eyes and beak with vodka and food color.

Design by Clau-
dette Tidwell,
Nashville, TN

Design: Claudette Tidwell
Nashville, Tennessee

This cute little bird nest molded of marzipan with colorful marzipan eggs would be appropriate for Easter or any spring event.

The Kentucky Derby is acknowledged throughout the world, but in Kentucky the first Saturday in May is recognized in celebrity style from the "Thunder Over Louisville" fireworks, numerous gala parties, to race day itself. From the race of thoroughbred horses running for the "roses" to the female attendees decked in fabulous designer hats, this is a colorful and unforgettable Kentucky event.

Derby Winner

The star of the Derby is the equestrian thoroughbred, so it seems only fitting that we open the May chapter with a cupcake replica of a horse large enough to serve about three dozen guests.

Supplies
- Horse head pattern
- Horse head-shaped cake board cut to shape
- 3 dozen standard cupcakes
- Chocolate butter cream, approximately 4 pounds
- 1 white gum ball
- Tip #3 and decorator bag
- Smooth paper towels
- Fondant in red, green and white
- Black butter cream

Arrange cup
cakes on horse
shape board

Double the size of the horse head pattern in the back of this book. Allow a half inch around the pattern and cut the base board to the contour of the head. Leaving the paper on the cupcakes in tack, arrange the standard size cupcakes to cover the contoured board, attaching each with a dab of frosting.

Generously cover the entire cupcake ensemble with the brown chocolate frosting covering only the tops and not the side edges of the cupcakes. Smooth the frosting with a spatula let it air dry then smooth and contour it with a paper towel.

Generously frost the cup cakes

Use a white gum ball for the eye

Add red halter

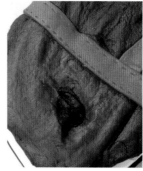

Fill in the nostril with black

The nostril, ears, and front of the face have deeper contours than other areas of the head. Press a white gumball into the eye area and smooth the eye lids around it. Roll a small black ball of fondant and flatten it into an oval for the pupil of the eye. Use the remainder of the black to fill in the nostril.

Roll a long log of red fondant and cut it into 1 inch wide strips and position them for the halter.

Fill a decorator bag with a #3 or larger writing tip and black butter cream. Pipe lines from the back edge of the neck and down onto the face to form the black mane.

The winning Derby horse is awarded the coveted blanket of red roses around his neck so, to follow tradition, we can add several beautiful red gum paste roses around the neck of the winner.

Follow the rose directions in chapter 6, "June Bride," to create the flowers. Fill in the spaces with fondant leaves or pipe them in the opening with a leaf tip and green butter cream. This creation is perfect for your Derby party or any equestrian lovers event.

Pipe a black #3 mane

Red roses around the neck

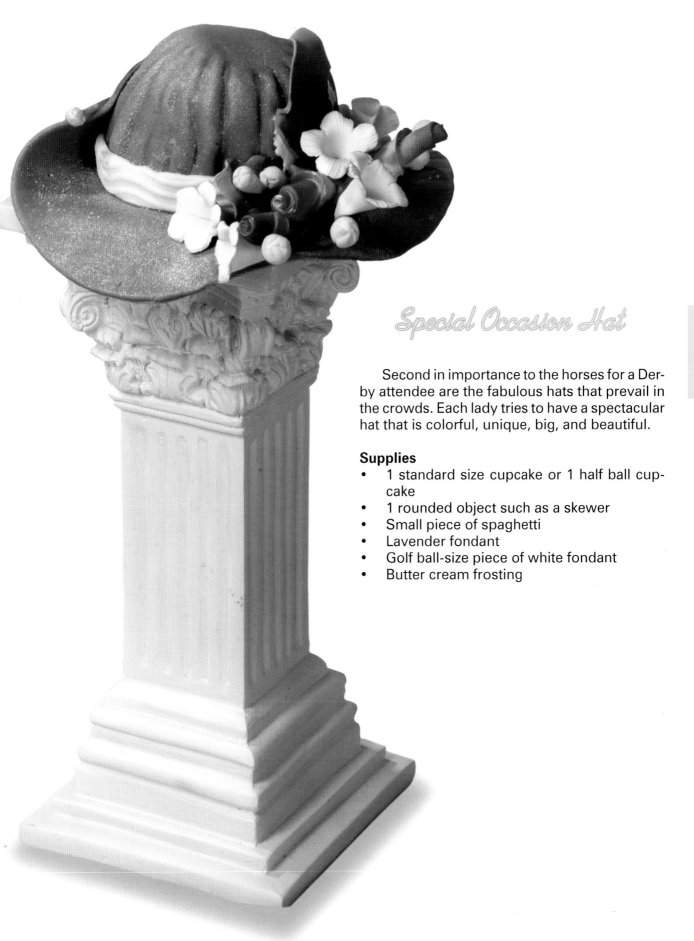

Special Occasion Hat

Second in importance to the horses for a Derby attendee are the fabulous hats that prevail in the crowds. Each lady tries to have a spectacular hat that is colorful, unique, big, and beautiful.

Supplies
- 1 standard size cupcake or 1 half ball cupcake
- 1 rounded object such as a skewer
- Small piece of spaghetti
- Lavender fondant
- Golf ball-size piece of white fondant
- Butter cream frosting

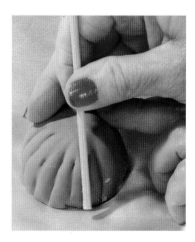

Use a 1/2 ball cake or trim a standard cup cake

Cover the cup cake with fondant

Press vertical grooves

Frost the half ball cake or trim a standard cupcake without the paper to the appropriate shape. Cover the frosted cupcake with thinly rolled lavender fondant. Use a skewer or the rounded handle of a paint brush to make vertical, grooved impressions around the crown of the hat.

Form the brim

Place cup cake in center of brim

To form the brim of the hat, roll a large piece of lavender fondant and cut a 4 inch circle. Place the cupcake on the center of the round brim. Cut a 1/4 inch strip of white fondant and wrap it around the connection of the hat and the brim. Roll one side of the brim up and attach it against the side of the crown of the hat.

Push a 1-1/2 inch piece of spaghetti through the soft hat brim and add a small fondant ball on one end of the spaghetti. Brush the "pin" with silver luster and the white ball with pearl luster to create the appearance of a large hat pin.

Select an arrangement of small purchased flowers and secure them on the opposite side of the brim with some frosting. If you are not planning a Derby party, this feminine hat would be perfect for Mothers Day or even mom's birthday. Each guest will be thrilled at their individual confection.

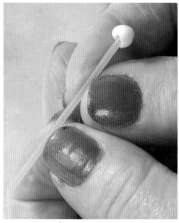

Add white hat band

Form hat pin from spaghetti

Add floral arrangement to hat

Cinco de Mayo

In tribute to our Spanish friends and heritage the fifth day of May, known as Cinco De Mayo, is a historic event and a day of celebration. With this in mind, this favorite "tres leche" or three milk cake is a perfect treat for the special day.

supplies
- 6 egg yolks
- 2 cups granulated sugar
- 1 Tablespoon vanilla
- 1/2 cup milk
- 2 cups self-rising flour
- 6 egg whites
- 1 can condensed milk
- 1 can evaporated milk
- 1 cup heavy cream
- 1 ½ cup beaten egg whites
- 1/4 cup water
- 2 ¼ cup granulated sugar
- whipped cream
- stemmed cherries

This cake is normally baked in an 8 inch x 13 inch pan but for our individual treats we are baking them as standard size cupcakes. Mix together the first four ingredients then add all of the flour. Beat the egg whites until stiff then fold into the previous ingredients by hand. Bake approximately 15 minutes at 350 degrees or until firm when touched.

Remove papers and place cup cakes in parfait glass

Frost with Italian Meringue

Pour three milks over the cup cakes

Garnish with whipped cream

Remove the papers from three cupcakes. Place one into a parfait or desert glass, pressing it firmly into the bottom of the glass. Add a layer of Italian Meringue frosting. To make this frosting, boil 1/4 cup water with 2-1/4 cup granulated sugar. Boil together for several minutes until all sugar crystals are dissolved. Pour this hot mixture slowly into 1-1/2 cup beaten egg whites and blend slowly with a mixer. Add another cupcake, a layer of frosting and the top layer.

Mix together the three milks and pour generously over the cupcakes until they are thoroughly soaked.

Frost the parfait with Italian Meringue. Top the frosting with a generous topping of whipped cream. Add a stemmed cherry to complete the luscious desert.

Design: Alexandria Pappas
Nashville, Tennessee

When spring arrives the ball teams explode from T-Ball, little league, soft ball, to base ball — all perfect occasions for these theme cupcakes. The lacing on this baseball is created with cut pieces of a candy called *Cherry Twizzl*ers. A ball bat can be formed from a pretzel stick covered with brown fondant to complete the theme. A baseball cap could be made in a king size cupcake.

Design: Susan Zugehoer
Hebron, Kentucky

White frosting and tip # 104 are used to pipe the petals of this delicate daisy. A circle of yellow gum paste is cut and sprinkled with yellow sugar for the center of the flower. A tray of pastel color daisies would be perfect for a garden party or spring tea.

Design: Susan Zugehoer
Hebron, Kentucky

This colorful flower could be used as a black-eyed Susan or a chrysanthemum by using a tip # 104 to form circular rows of petals. Either pipe a brown center or cut a circle of brown gum paste.

52

Design: Christine Clark
Cincinnati, Ohio

This beautiful little wishing well took first place in the cupcake division at the Queen City Cake Show in Cincinnati, Ohio.

Design: Diane Constant
LaGrange, Kentucky

To form the petite flower pot, Diane wrapped a real pot with clear plastic wrap to mold her terra cotta colored fondant. When the fondant dried, she removed the pot and plastic wrap to allow the pot to finish drying. Two standard cupcakes are frosted and placed in the pot. Chocolate cookie crumbs form the dirt. The daisy is formed in a gum paste daisy mold. The tiny picture could be an eatable image to make everything entirely edible or it could be a cut out snap shot. The banner and leaves are free formed and the stem can be a dowel or a pretzel stick covered with green fondant.

Design: Beth Parvu
South Bend, Indiana
Photo: Lou Putnam
South Bend, Indiana

Tiny gum paste fairies frolic in this cupcake rose garden to assure the beauty of spring. Fairies are formed with an Angela cutter found on Beth's web site. The beautiful, natural roses are formed of gum paste then brushed with several layers of deep red velvet crystal dusting powder over-layered with burgundy. The leaf borders are also gum paste that are cut, veined, and dusted with shades of green dusting powder. Necessary supplies are available at www.sugarpaste.com

Design courtesy Vicky Harlen, Abbeville, SC

Design: Vicky Harlen
Abbeville, South Carolina

Use an ISAC patchwork quilt cutter to make a yellow fondant blanket and place it over an iced cupcake. Use Sweet Expressions Baby molds to make the bear and block from fondant. Detail with colored food pens and or petal dusts. Place the bear on the blanket with a little butter cream frosting and spray with pearl dust.

Design: Darlene Nold
Louisville, Kentucky

This little clutch bag would be charming for any occasion but especially Mother's Day. Two cupcakes form the base with a third sitting on them to give the height to the purse. Remove the papers and frost the cupcake ensemble. Roll long, thin strips of black fondant and gather to form the rows of ruffles. Brightly colored polka dots are cut from the large end of a decorator tip. A plastique mold of an actual purse clasp was made to form the gum paste version which is edged with a row of edible pearls.

Design courtesy Darlene Nold, Louisville, KY

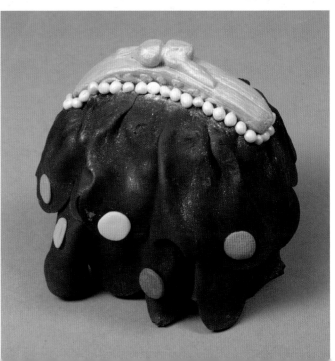

Design: Angie Thacker
Groveport, Ohio

The lovely pink dragonfly was created by Angie as a Mother's Day tribute to her mother and best friend, Helen Elizabeth Gilliam (1950-2007). The dragonfly was made from fondant, allowed to dry overnight, and dusted with pearl luster. To form the wings, roll out two logs of fondant, about three inches long and the diameter of a dime. Roll a thin layer of black fondant, cut two rectangles about 2-1/2 inches wide and 3 inches long, and brush a little water onto one black rectangle. Place a log onto the black piece and roll it up, repeating the process for the second log. Allow to dry for a few minutes then pinch the logs on one side to flatten. Attach one cane on top of the other and allow it to dry. Use a sharp knife to cut thin strips of the cane to form beautiful dragonfly wings. When dry, add to the cake with a little icing and top with the dragonfly. For the flowered lettering, cut small gumpaste flowers. Cut small circles for the centers and stamp with food color or use a food writer pen.

Design: Brenda Hoye
West Jefferson, Ohio
Photo: Christine Clark
Cincinnati, Ohio

Brenda has incorporated cupcakes into this beautiful tea set arrangement to make a stunning presentation. Two of the cupcakes are covered with tiny gum paste flowers. All pieces are crafted of gum paste and hand painted.

Tea Set design courtesy of Brenda Hoye, West Jefferson, OH. Photo courtesy of Christine Clark, Cincinnati, OH

June is the traditional month for weddings with all the frills, flowers, and anticipation that goes into the preparations for the perfect event of a life time. Amid all the hustle and bustle of new marriages, be careful not to forget the man who is paying the bills – dear old dad! Fathers Day is the perfect occasion to tell Dad how much you appreciate and love him with a special cupcake creation.

June Bride

Frosting ruffles, laser cut lace, and blushing pink rosebuds set the theme for the most meticulous June bride.

Supplies
- Two dozen standard cupcakes
- Plexiglas cake stand using 6 inch, 8 inch, and 10 inch plates
- 41 gum paste roses and 82 leaves
- 24 laser cut cupcake wrappers
- Ruffle tip # 415
- Gum paste cutters for rose petal and leaf

Steps to form roses

Steps to form leaves

Roses can be formed well in advance but allow at least overnight for drying. You will need 41 small rose buds and one larger open rose for the top of the arrangement. To form the center of each rose, make a small cone shape from fondant or other paste that you are using. Roll a thin piece of pink paste and cut 3 petals. Brush the lower half of each with gum glue. Wrap the first petal around the top of the cone. It will extend above the top of the cone. Soften the edges of the second and third petal on a cel pad with a ball tool. Add the second and third petal, overlapping each slightly.

Cut green leaves with a rose leaf cutter. The pictured cutter will also incorporate the veins. Lay the leaves in a flower former to curve slightly. When the leaves are dry, brush them with pearl luster to highlight each. You need two leaves for each rose on a cupcake and one leaf for each rose on the plate.

Pipe ruffles around cup cake

Place cup cake in laser cut cup

Bake and cool two dozen cupcakes. Place a #415 decorator tip into a decorator bag with white butter cream frosting. Pipe a ruffle around the circumference of a cupcake. Repeat for the second ruffle, slightly overlapping the first. Add a third row of ruffles to finish the top. Place a rose bud and two leaves in the center of each cupcake. Wrap each with a white laser-cut plastic wrapper and fasten. Arrange the completed cupcakes on the plates of a Plexiglas stand. More plates and layers could be added but additional supports on the pictured stand are hidden by the drape at the base. Add a leaf and rosebud between each cupcake and attach to the plate with a touch of butter cream frosting. One large pink open rose sets on the top layer on the ensemble as the finishing touch.

Laser cut plastic wrapper

Romance

Candlelight and red roses set the romantic ambiance of this tiered cupcake centerpiece designed for a "simply elegant" wedding.

Supplies

- Three dozen standard cupcakes
- Foam core board
- Two mirrors – 10 inch and 12 inch
- Votive candles
- Rose stencil
- Royal frosting – red and green
- 5-1/2 pounds fondant – 5 lb white and 1/2 lb red
- Ribbon or pizza cutter
- Ribbon drying rack
- Embossing roller
- Bead maker

Form the bow in advance, using the 1/2 pound of red fondant or gum paste. Roll a well kneaded ball on a surface that is lightly coated with powdered sugar. Roll the fondant until it is very thin but thick enough to hold together when you lift the sheet.

For textured designs place the design roller in center of the thin sheet of fondant and roll to each end. It is best to use the palm of your hand to apply pressure to the roller in order to achieve a clearer pattern. To create the look of grooved, grosgrain ribbon, I have used a 12 inch x 1/2 inch piece of all thread, purchased from a hardware or home repair shop. Before using wash and dry thoroughly. Any impression roller can be used to create various ribbon patterns.

Use a ribbon cutter with a 1 inch spacer or a pizza cutter to cut horizontal strips of ribbon. Cut these strips to form 4 inch long lengths. Lift each strip and wrap it around a ribbon drying rack. Slightly dampen one end of the loop and press the ends together with your fingertips to secure it around the pipe. Repeat the process until you have at least 24 loops for each bow. It is always better to make a few extra loops to allow for breakage. Check the loops occasionally to be sure that they

Form ribbon loops

Use the loops to build the bow.

are not sticking to the pipe. Allow the loops to dry overnight, then remove from the rack by sliding the loops off of the end of the pipe.

Make a base for the bow by rolling a small ball of fondant to 1/8 inch thickness. Cut a circle with a large jar lid or other cutter that is approximately 2-1/2 to 3 inch diameter. Place the circle on a sheet of waxed paper and allow it to dry while the loops are drying.

To assemble, leave the base on the waxed paper and spread a thick coat of red royal frosting over the base. Place a ring of loops around the base edge so that the ends are secure in the royal frosting and the loops extend over the edge of the base. Place a mound of royal in the center of the ring of loops. Add a second ring of loops on top of the first ring, alternating the loops so that they are positioned between the loops of the first row. The first row of loops lays flat on the base but each additional row is elevated. Add another mound of frosting in the center and continue adding rings of loops until the bow is full and fluffy. Set the bow aside and allow it to dry before removing the waxed paper. The loops will accumulate a powdered sugar coating during the formation process. To remove this sugar and to intensify the color, brush each loop with vodka or other high alcoholic beverage. Alcohol will evaporate quickly and leave a shine whereas water would cause the gum paste to become sticky.

Cut cake board

Place cup cakes on shaped board

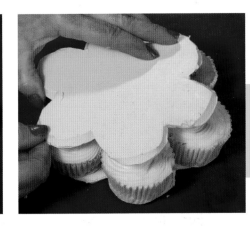

Lay second board on top of cup cakes

Draw around a 6-inch cake pan to form a round circle on a piece of foam core board. Place cupcakes around the edge of the circle and draw a line where they form scallops on the outside of the circle. Cut out the scalloped circle with a sharp knife. Lay the completed pattern on another piece of foam board and cut another identical board. Use the same process to make two 8-inch scalloped boards, this time setting eight cupcakes around the edge of an 8-inch circle.

Place a dot of frosting on each of seven cupcakes, leaving the papers on, and arrange them on one of the 6-inch boards placing six around the edge and one in the center. Frost the entire top of the cupcakes as if they were one cake. Lay the second scalloped 6 inch board on top of the cupcakes. If you do not want the board to touch the frosting of the lower row, you can add small dowel supports onto the bottom side of the top board.

Place cup cakes on top board

Place 7 additional cupcakes on the top board and frost the top with butter cream. If you have any cracks or crevices on the sides, fill them in with butter cream so that the surface will be smooth.

Roll out a circle of white fondant that is large enough to cover the top and sides of the cupcake arrangement. It should be approximately 14 inch diameter – 6 inch across the top and 4 inch for each side. Drape the fondant over the cupcakes and smooth across the top and into the crevices of each scallop. Trim any excess around the base of the cake.

Spread frosting on stencil

Stenciled rose

Mix 1/2 cup red royal frosting and 1/2 cup green. Position a plastic rose stencil tightly against the front of one scallop. Using an off set spatula and red royal, spread the frosting across the cut out rose pattern of the stencil, removing all excess frosting. Gently lift the stencil from the cake to expose the perfect red rose. Repeat the process on the remaining scallops. Allow the rose to dry to the touch.

Place the stencil in place once again and spread green frosting over the stem and leaf cut out pattern of the stencil. Remove the stencil and continue to add stems for all of the roses. Frequently check to see that there is no excess frosting on the back of the stencil as this will cause a smear of the pattern.

Repeat the process for the 8 inch cake. Additional larger ensembles can be created to accommodate any size crowd.

Place the cake on a 10-inch mirror. Mold a thin strip of white fondant into a silicone bead maker. Remove the strip gently and place it around the base of the cake as a border. Two lengths will encircle the 6 inch cake. You may need to pipe a thin line of butter cream around the cake before adding the beads to secure the border into place. Brush the border with pearl luster.

Cut several 1 inch wide ribbon streamers of various lengths to hand over the edge of the cake. Be sure to impress the streamers with the same pattern as the bow. Place the bow on top of the cake. For an elegant arrangement, use glass blocks to form various display levels. Votive candles or twinkle lights add a reflective romantic touch on the glass blocks.

Make pearls in bead maker

Place bow on top of arrangement

Rack Them Up

Although this design would make a perfect groom's cake for the avid billiards fan, it can also reflect Dad's favorite hobby for a special Fathers Day treat.

Supplies
- 16 standard cupcakes
- 12 inch x 12 inch x 12 inch foam core board triangle
- 16 inch x 16 inch x 16 inch covered cake board
- Butter cream frosting
- 1/2 pound fondant divided into black and white
- 1/2 pound fondant divided into golf ball size red, blue, green, orange, yellow
- Ribbon or pizza cutter
- Food safe markers
- Round 3 inch cutter
- Medium size decorator tip & #18 tip

Frost cup cakes with rounded tops

Cut fondant circles for tops of balls

Bake and cool cupcakes. It is helpful if the cupcakes bake with a rounded top but if not, pipe and mound frosting with a #18 tip to give each an even rounded top.

Roll out a piece of white fondant and cut 7 circles with the 3 inch cutter. Lay the circle over a frosted cupcake and gently stretch and rub until the rounded top reaches the cupcake paper.

Place fondant on frosted cup cake

Select a pool ball color, such as red, and roll it out. Cut a circle with the round cutter and place over a cupcake. Roll the remainder of the red very thin and cut a 1 inch wide strip with the ribbon cutter. Lay the 1 inch strip of red over the center of a white cupcake and slightly dampen it to secure. Trim the ends at the top edge of the cupcake paper.

Roll a small piece of white fondant very thin and cut 15 circles with the large end of a decorator tip. Attach one circle to the top of each ball. Repeat the process until all of the pool balls are covered with the correct color and number. Apply a small amount of butter cream to the bottom of each cupcake and arrange on the foam core triangle. Place the foam board onto a stronger cake board.

Write numbers on each ball with the appropriate color food marker. If you do not have access to food safe markers, you can write the numbers with a tiny paint brush and food color.

Write numbers on small white circles

Cut three strips of black fondant 15 inch long x 2 inch wide x 1/8 inch thick for the pool rack. Allow these pieces to dry overnight. Pipe a line of black royal around the edge of the board and stand the pieces on their edge in the frosting. It may be necessary to prop the pieces in a standing position until they dry.

The solid white cue ball can lay to the side of the pool rack when displayed.

Pool rack

Design: Leigh Sipe
Harrodsburg, Kentucky

It takes 105 jumbo cupcakes to fill this custom built stand. The two layer 5 inch cake on top is frosted and covered with a chocolate wrap design. Each of the 105 strawberries is swirled in white/brown melted chocolate. The bride and groom top pieces are strawberries. The bride is dipped in white with a tulle veil. The groom is dipped in chocolate with a tiny plastic top hat and cane. With a few alterations this ensemble is perfect for any large crowd. The pink and white swirled dipped strawberries on the second cake made a spectacular creation for a special 100th birthday.

63

Design: Alexandria Pappas
Nashville, Tennessee

This miniature three-tier wedding cake is constructed on a jumbo, a standard, and a mini cupcake. A #20 decorator tip is used for the borders and a #3 tip for the dots. Tiny gum paste flowers are cut out and arranged for the top piece. These small cakes are very popular as individual table treats for the wedding guests.

Design: Anna Johnson
Louisville, Kentucky

A jumbo, a standard, and a mini cupcake are carved and stacked to create this adorable miniature topsy-turvy wedding cake. The layers are covered with bright pink fondant and trimmed with a vivid yellow. Tiny cut out gum paste or fondant flowers are clustered for the top arrangement.

Design: Mary Burton
Crown Point, Indiana

This delightful little tool box is formed from a mini loaf-size cake covered with brown fondant or frosting. Sugar lay-on tools complete this treat which is sure to please any handyman.

Design: Alexandria Pappas
Nashville, Tennessee

A jumbo cupcake is used to create this scrumptious miniature groom's cake. A #47 and a #20 tip are used with chocolate frosting to pipe borders and side designs. The cluster of grapes on top of the creation consists of tiny chocolate purchased candies.

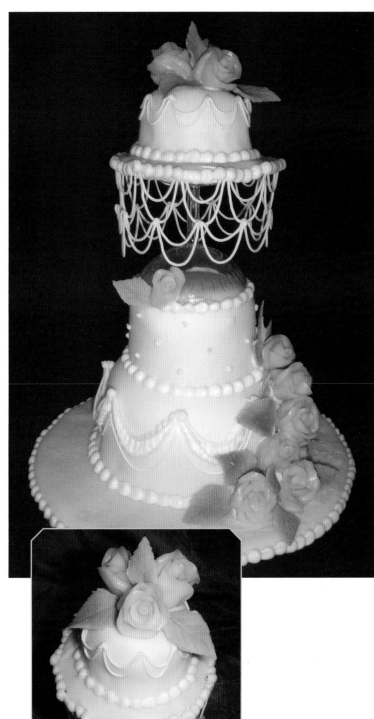

Design & photo Bob Holsinger
Colorado Springs, Colorado

This delicate wedding cake favor is created from 1 jumbo, 1 standard and 1 mini size cupcake and covered with fondant. The tier separators are small size plastic champagne glasses which are often used as favors. Base borders are from a #3 tip and all the fragile string work between the tiers is piped with a #1 tip. Bob actually designs large wedding cakes in this style and transports them in tact, rarely breaking a single string.

Design & photo: Bob Holsinger,
Colorado Springs, Colorado

This three-tier cake is also a jumbo, a standard and a mini cupcake stacked together with only one separator, a small plastic champagne glass. The cascade of roses is hand-molded of pink fondant and leaves are cut from a very small cutter and veined.

Celebrate the Flag

The mention of July brings to mind Independence Day, fireworks, celebrations and patriotism. The red, white and blue of our flag signify our independence and freedom.

Supplies
- 32 – 36 mini cupcakes
- Red and blue fondant
- White butter cream
- White stars from assorted candy stars

Frost the flag with white butter cream

Prepare a 9 inch x 12 inch base board. Cut a cake board using the enclosed pattern. Attach the cake pattern to the board with frosting and arrange the mini cupcakes to the shape of a waving flag, leaving the papers intact.

Cover the entire top of the flag with white butter cream. Add extra frosting vertically where the flag folds so that you can smooth and contour the fold with a paper towel to resemble a waving flag.

Blue background

Add blue to upper left corner

Thinly roll a piece of blue fondant and cut a piece 3-1/2 inch tall and 4-1/2 inch long. Add this blue to the upper left corner of the flag. Select white stars from the assorted jar and add rows of stars to the flag.

Cut 7 red stripes approximately 1/2 inch wide each and add them to the flag, beginning and ending with a red stripe.

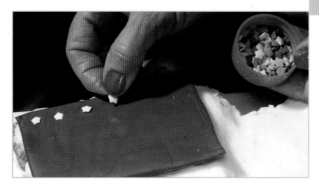

Add white stars

Add red stripes

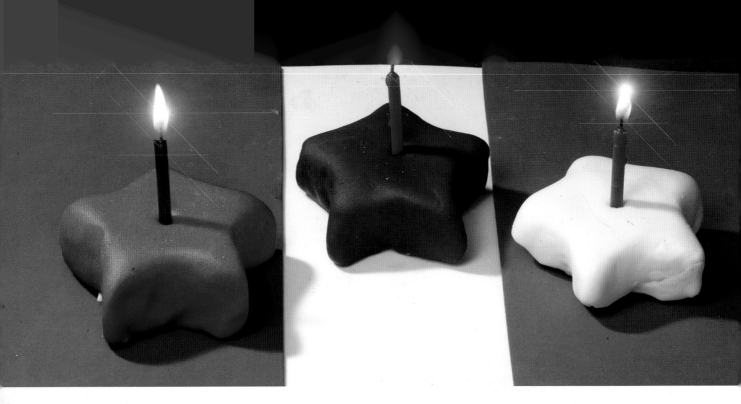

Liberty Stars

In different colors these little stars would be appropriate for various occasions such as a diva star, star athletic, birthday star, or even a Christmas star, but when decorated in red, white and blue they are undisputedly a sign of United States freedom. Add a sparkler candle on each star and you have the perfect desert for your 4th of July fireworks celebration.

Remove from pan

Supplies
- Star shape disposable cupcake pans
- Frosting, red, white and blue either butter cream or fondant
- Sparkler candles

Bake and cool star shape cupcakes. Remove the disposable pans and invert the cakes so the bottom baked side is facing up.

Cover each cake with red, white or blue frosting and display it on a patriot tray. Insert a sparkler candle in each and light shortly before serving.

Cover with frosting

68

Uncle Sam's Hat

Uncle Sam's tall, red, white, and blue hat is quickly recognized as a symbol of patriotism and freedom.

Supplies
- 2 standard cupcakes
- Red, white and blue fondant
- Candy stars
- butter cream

Stack 2 cup cakes

Frost stacked cup cakes

Remove the paper wrappers from 2 standard cupcakes and attach one on top of the other with frosting. Frost the top and sides of the stacked cakes with white butter cream and smooth with a paper towel.

Cut eleven 1/2 inch red fondant strips that will reach from the base to the top edge of the stacked ensemble. Roll a large piece of white for the hat brim and cut a 4 inch circle.

Add red stripes

Roll hat brim

Add stars to hat band

Place the tall part of the hat onto the center of the 4 inch circle. Cut a half inch strip of blue fondant and wrap the band where the two pieces join to hide the connection. Attach numerous sugar stars to the hat band. Place a hat onto desert plates to serve as individual treats.

Add hat band to hat

Design: Vera Gooch
 Kings Mountain, Kentucky

The striking color combination of this black fondant-covered mini cake and the shocking hot pink of the gumpaste flower makes this a miniature work of art. Each petal of the fantasy flower is cut and dried before assembling. Delicate royal string work adorns the base of the treat. This would be a great entry for a cupcake competition.

70

Design: Kathy Scott
Abbeville, South Carolina

All of these cupcakes were iced in butter cream and several designs also have fondant. Kathy rolled out fondant in white and different shades of green. She then rolled them with a textured roller. She used a round cutter slightly larger than the cupcake and placed the cutout circle on top of the butter cream frosted cupcake. If your icing has set up, you can spray the tops with water so the fondant will adhere.

The flowers are fondant using silicone molds (available from Kathy). Press the fondant firmly in the mold being careful not to overfill. Let the fondant sit in the mold five to ten minutes. For deeper more intricate molds or to speed the process, you can put the molds in the freezer. If you use the freezer method let the fondant come back to room temperature before painting. Kathy colored fondant appropriate to the flowers and used an airbrush to add details. She added fondant leaves where needed and dusted all the cupcakes using an airbrush.

Molds used for the flowers are Sweet Express molds: F18, F1, F17, F50, F7, F31, F66, F22, F3, F10, F93, F111, F19, and F39. Available at www.sweetexpress.com

The August cupcake selection depicts several of the expectations of summer such as fishing trips, adventures at the beach and the flavors of summers produce.

Just Peachy

One of the most mouthwatering treats of summer is the luscious peach plucked fresh from the tree.

Supplies
- 2 standard or 2 half ball cupcakes for each peach
- Piping gel
- Yellow butter cream
- Dry Jell-O in orange, peach, cherry
- A small ball of Plastique molding material
- Walnut size ball of white fondant
- Off-set spatula
- Touch of red food color

72

To form a whole peach, use frosting to fasten 2 half balls or 2 standard cupcakes, with the paper removed, together. Cover the 2 pieces with a generous amount of light yellow frosting to form a round peach.

Fasten 2 halves together

Frost with light yellow frosting

Open the three packages of Jell-o, peach, orange and cherry, and pour about one half of each box into a flat pan. While the butter cream is still damp, roll the "peach" cake in the dry Jell-o. Make sure that you get some of each color. Continue to roll in the peach flavor. This will give the textured surface of peach fuzz as well as the peach aroma. Indent a small groove at the top to represent the stem area and mark the crease with a skewer or dull knife where the two halves connect.

Roll in dry Jell-o

Mark the crease

If you plan to form the peach halves, you will need to form the peach seed in advance. Select a walnut size ball of white plastique and a ball of blue plastique. Blend the two colors until they are all blue. Take a real peach seed that you have previously saved and press it firmly into the plastique. Leave the seed in the mold for several hours before removing it to reveal a perfect seed mold.

Press seed into Plastique

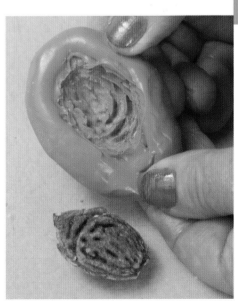

Remove peach seed

Press fondant into mold

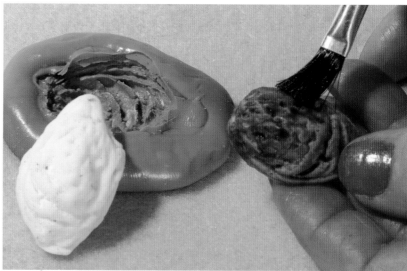

Remove seed and color

Roll a walnut-size piece of white fondant until it is smooth. Press the piece firmly into the mold. Gently remove the seed and place the grooved design face up to dry. When the seed is dry, brush it generously with a thinned mixture of brown and terra cotta so that the color has sort of a rusty appearance.

Prepare the halves as you did the whole peach. Coat the entire surface with light yellow butter cream. Press an indention in each half where the seed will be.

Roll the outside of each half in the three flavors of dry Jell-o. Do not coat the inside of the halves. Press the seed into one peach half. Brush the seed indention of the second half with thinned red gel color. Coat the inside of both halves, including the seed, with clear piping gel. Your creation will not only look like fresh peaches but they will smell like them because of the peach Jell-o.

Brush halves with piping gel

Gone Fishing

This prize catch is sure to delight the avid fisherman. This great reminder of the summer vacation is formed from one mini loaf cake.

Supplies
- 1 mini loaf pan
- fondant – gray, green and white
- fish pattern
- 1 decorator tip
- Small pieces of spaghetti

Carve mini loaf cake

Bake and cool a mini loaf cake for each fish. Carve it to fit the included pattern. Frost the cake with thinned butter cream to secure all of the cut edges and crumbs. Allow the piece to air dry.

To form the fins, roll a small piece of white fondant. Lay the enclosed patterns on the fondant and cut them out with a small, pointed knife. Insert short pieces of spaghetti into the soft fins to support the pieces on the cake. Curve the tail to dry. Cut and cover a foam core board to the shape of the fish. Cover the board with foil.

Forming fins

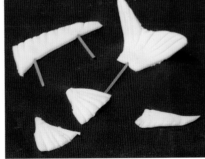

Cover board

Cover with blended fondant

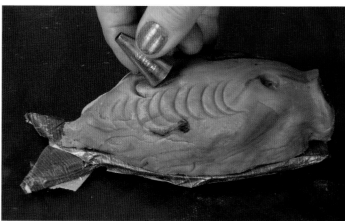

Impress scales

Use walnut-size balls of dark green, gray, and white fondant to roll out together. The green should be used for the top of the fish and the white used for the stomach. Roll the blended fondant out to a thin consistency and drape over the fish.

Use the large end of a decorator tip to mark rows of scales. Press an indentation for the eye and place a small ball of fondant into the groove. Add a black pupil for the eye.

Cut a semi-circle and lift it slightly to insert a small strip of red fondant for the gill.

Attach the fins in their proper positions using a little frosting and the spaghetti you previously inserted. Brush the fish lightly with green pearl luster to give it a glossy, wet look.

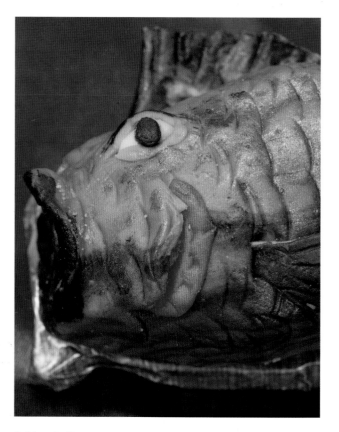

Add red gills

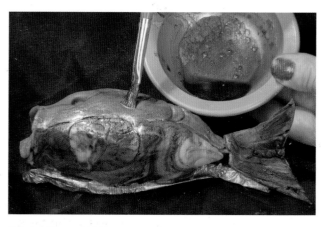

Paint with pearl luster

Pink Flamingo

The sight of the beautiful pink flamingo in the blue and green of the Florida Everglades makes a person truly aware of the beauty of summer.

Supplies
- 1 Styrofoam ball
- Blue butter cream
- 1 egg shape cupcake
- Fondant – pink and yellow
- Pink butter cream
- Black food pen
- 1 wooden skewer

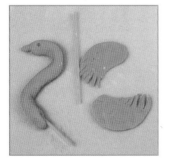

Form base and legs

Form body

Steps to form wings and neck

To form the base for the flamingo, cut a Styrofoam ball or egg shape in half vertically. Glue the flat side of one half to the base with hot glue and allow it to set.

Trim the second half on each side to create an egg shape which will form the stomach of the flamingo.

Cover the 5 inch skewers with yellow fondant for the legs. Insert the straight yellow skewers or flamingo legs into the base Styrofoam. Place the second egg shape Styrofoam onto the top of the leg.

With a 5 inch log of hot pink fondant, shape the neck, head and beak. Allow the neck to dry overnight. To form the wings, use a round cutter that has a 1-1/2 inch diameter. Cut two circles and stretch them to elongate. Trim a curve from the upper side and cut feathers with small scissors.

Cut an egg-shape cake board from foam core board and attach an egg-shape cupcake with frosting. Place the cupcake on top of the base and frost the entire body with hot pink butter cream or rolled butter cream. Smooth the frosting with a paper towel.

Attach the neck to the flamingo. It may be necessary to push a short skewer thru the neck into the foam base to hold it into position until the frosting sets. Place the wings on either side and secure them with frosting.

Use a black food safe writer pen to form a black dot on either side for the eyes. Frost the board with blue to represent water.

Sea Shells

The beach is always a favorite spot to vacation. These chocolate sea shells can serve as a reminder of anticipation before you take the trip or a happy memory of the fun time you had after you return home.

Supplies
- Sea shell candy mold
- White chocolate
- Small amount of milk chocolate
- Pearl luster
- A standard cupcake
- Brown or raw sugar for sand

Remove shells from mold

Brush shells with pearl luster   Arrange shells on cup cake

Bake and cool standard cupcakes. While they are cooling, form the sea shells. Melt the white chocolate in one container and the milk chocolate in another. Fill the mold cavities with white. Blend and swirl a touch of the brown chocolate with a toothpick. Place the mold in the refrigerator to set. When the shells are thoroughly cooled, invert the mold and remove the shells.

Brush each shell with pearl luster and arrange the shells on a cupcake that has been frosted with butter cream. Sprinkle brown or raw sugar to give the cupcake a hint of sand.

Susan Zugehoer
Hebron, Kentucky

During the heat of August, this colorful sun cupcake is sure to be the hit of the summer picnic or day at the beach. Frost the cupcake light yellow and place pieces of candy corn around the edge to represent rays of the sun. Add candy eyes and mouth for the facial features.

Design: Falencia Frazier
Cincinnati, Ohio
Photo: by Christine Clark
Cincinnati, OH

Either a jumbo cupcake or a ball shape cupcake could be used to form the body of this playful little clown. Cover the entire cupcake to resemble clothing and add a small ball of fondant or a gum ball for the head and add features. A great idea for a child's party.

Design: Bonnie Blackburn
Feversham, Ontario, Canada

These fishing cupcakes are formed by frosting one side of the cupcake blue and the other side green, using a grass tip to pipe some grass. Frost Teddy Grahams to look like they are wearing tee shirts and shorts. Add Black sunglasses on some and baseball caps on others using a #4 tip so they look like swimmers and let dry. Line up goldfish crackers on a paper towel and spray with an airbrush. Spray about 15 blue on both sides and the next 15 spray with red, yellow, green and purple. Let the fish dry over night. Use a needle and black thread to pull the thread through the eye of the fish and tie onto the end of pretzel sticks. Proceed with the remaining fish. Stand a decorated teddy bear and pretzel on the green side of each cupcake. Arrange some fish and drop flowers on the cupcakes.

79

Leigh Sipe
Harrodsburg, Kentucky

Cupcake mania has become so widespread that the influence is everywhere, including many special dishes and even fabric. Leigh has blended this segment of cupcakes to match ribbons, plates, fabric and even candles. The molded daisies seem to be an extension of the colorful plate; black polka dots blend into the candles, frosting and fabric; the black stripe design is perfect for the stripped ribbon that is looped through the cake plate and striped candles; the red lady bug from the background fabric seems to have leaped onto the top of the cake; the green grass and daisies complement the green plate; jumbo pastel cupcakes are copied from the cupcake print on the background fabric; and the Happy Birthday plate is surrounded with colorful frosted cupcakes complete with balloon birthday candles. Look around, the possibilities are endless. The ribbon plates are from a unique shop called "It's Personal" located in Lexington, Kentucky. If you want to cut corners you can use a scrap booking tool to form ribbon holes in a paper plate.

Design: Cecilia Morana
Buenos Aires
Photo: Maria Fernanda Morana

Cover muffins with rolled fondant of different colors of blue, yellow, red and orange. Stretch the gum paste and cut a circle for each car. With a cutter, cut an arc in each circle. Use water to stick each one to the cupcake. Model a rolled fondant sphere of the color of the car and cut it into two semi spheres. Stick them to the car, one in the front and the other in the back. Cut thin black gum paste strips and stick them to the circle of the base and to the car according to the picture. Form four black wheels for the car. Push into the center of each wheel with a ball modeling tool and paint the center with silver paste color. Attach the wheels to the car with royal frosting. Model the front and back lights of the car and attach them in place. Stretch gum paste and cut the numbers. Stick them on with water. The cars are ready for the race!!

Claudette Tidwell
Nashville, Tennessee

Everyone loves watermelon, so these miniature slices will be perfect for your special cookout or picnic. The slices are marzipan with luscious pink fruit complete with seeds.

82

SUMMER ENDS & SCHOOL BEGINS

Labor Day brings the close of summer with numerous picnics to enjoy the last days of summer before the school buses start running for another year of school

Labor Day Picnic

This little picnic basket crammed full of goodies is perfect for desert for your labor Day picnic.

Supplies
- 1 mini loaf pan cake
- 1 basket weave impression mat
- Brown fondant
- 2 saltine or graham crackers
- Butter cream frosting
- Candy runts

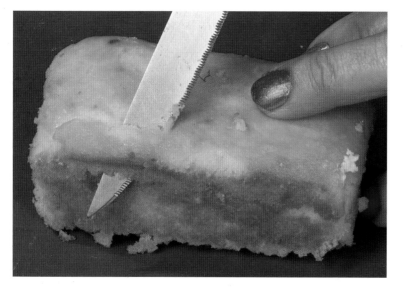

Trim mini loaf cake

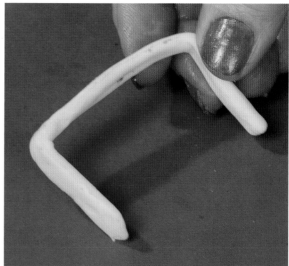

Shaping handle

Bake and cool mini loaf cakes. Trim the rounded top of the loaf to level and frost the cake with butter cream.

To form the handle, roll a 5 inch log of fondant. Flatten it and cut a 1/4 inch strip. Bend and dry the handle to shape. Let the handle dry overnight.

Roll a strip of brown fondant 11-1/2 inch long x 1-1/2 inch tall. Lay the piece in the impression mat and press firmly to impress the basket weave design into the fondant. Re-trim the strip to the proper size if it stretches and wrap it around the sides of the basket that has been coated with butter cream.

Impress fondant

Wrap fondant around basket

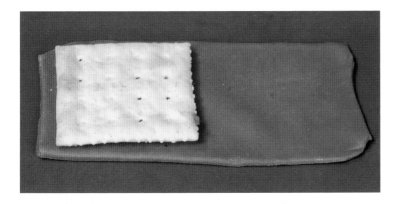

Forming lid

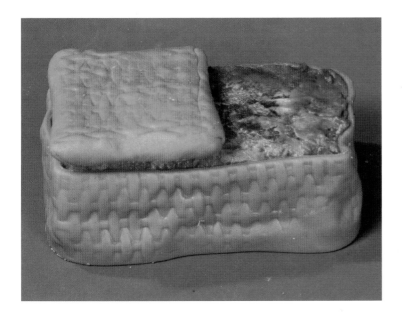

Lay lid on basket

Lay a cracker on a strip of embossed brown fondant and cover the top with the extended fondant strip. Press the fondant around all edges to seal and trim any excess. Repeat this process for the second lid.

Lay the first lid on one end of the basket top. Tilt the second lid and support it into an open position with a piece of spaghetti.

Fill all of the open cavity inside the basket with candy runts. The bananas and oranges are especially realistic. Form several grape clusters by rolling tiny balls of lavender fondant and forming them into cascading grapes. The grapes could also be formed with a decorator tip #2 and butter cream frosting. Place the finished baskets on a piece of red and white checked gingham to resemble a picnic table cloth.

Prop up one end of lid

Fill basket with candy

Hot Dog Treats

Another picnic treat is always the favorite hot dog. With these special creations, the kids can even have hot dogs for desert!

Supplies
- 1-1/4 mini loaf cakes for each treat
- Fondant or rolled butter cream
- Brown and terra cotta AmeriColor
- Light brown dusting powder

Cut one loaf in half

Cut into fourths

Bake and cool mini loaf cakes. Five little cakes will make four hot dogs. Cut one cake in half across the top and through the length of the cake. Allow the two halves to fall open like the halves of a bun.

Trim all edges to round them.

Cut the second cake in half the same as the first one. Next, cut each of these pieces in half lengthwise again to form four pieces.

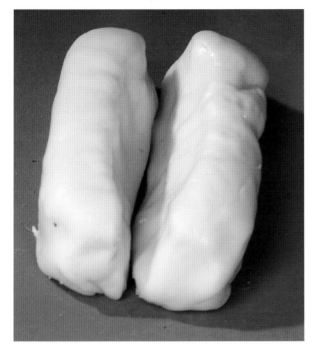

Cover bun with fondant

Cover hot dog with fondant

Roll out either white fondant or use rolled white butter cream and cover both halves of the "bun." Smooth the frosting to form the contour of a bun.

Color a piece of fondant or rolled butter cream with a mixture of brown and terra cotta food color. It should be blended to the shade of a real hot dog. Roll a rectanglur piece of the colored paste and place one of the small strips of cake onto the rectangle. Wrap the paste over it, pick it up, cover the cake and smooth into a hot dog.

Place the completed hot dog into the bun. Use light brown dusting powder mixed with a little pearl luster to brush shading onto the bun. Yellow butter cream can be piped on the hot dog to represent mustard.

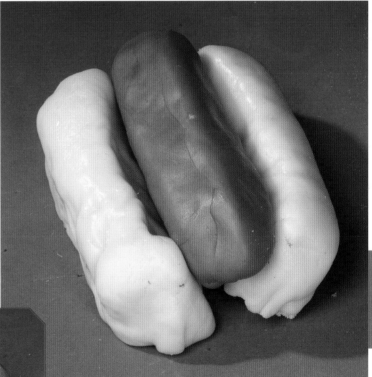

Place hot dog in bun

Dust with color

Back to School

The sight of school buses traveling the roads is a sure sign that the end of summer has arrived. These little buses would be perfect for a back to school party.

Supplies
- 1 mini loaf cake
- 4 chocolate mini mints
- Fondant – yellow, white and red
- #2 decorator tip
- Black butter cream or royal
- White butter cream

Bake, cool and frost a mini loaf with white butter cream. Cut a strip of white fondant 11-1/2 inches long and 1/4 inches tall. Wrap the piece around the top edge of the bus.

Cut a yellow strip of fondant that is 11-1/2 inches long by 1-1/4 inches tall. Place the yellow at the bottom edge of the white and wrap it around the cake. Cut a rectangle 4 inches long x 2 inches wide and place on top of the cake for the bus roof. Attach 2 of the chocolate mini mints to each side of the bus for wheels.

Roll tiny balls of red fondant to form lights for the appropriate areas on the bus. Two small flat ball are used for the headlights. Outline the division between the white and the yellow to conceal the connection. Make vertical black lines for form windows. Use the black tip to write the word "SCHOOL" on each side of the bus. You can also add your particular bus number or county to personalize your treats.

Flatten a small ball of red fondant to form the stop sign. Insert a short piece of spaghetti into the sign to insert it into the side of the bus.

Cut white fondant for windows

Cut yellow fondant for bus

Side of bus

Lights and wheels

Black outlines

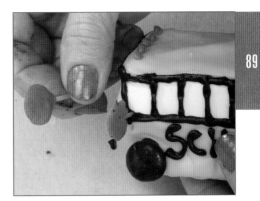
Inserting stop sign

Design: Leigh Sipe
Harrodsburg, Kentucky

The bears for this "beary" happy family are molded in First Impression bear molds. Papa bear has a yellow fondant vest and mama bear has a yellow dress. Baby boys have black ties and the girls wear yellow hair bows. The larger cupcake is unique because it actually uses a coffee filter for the paper and is baked in a 5 inch pan. Note that Leigh has used another ribbon plate along with a yellow tablecloth to pull the color theme together.

Design: Dathern Moon
Huntsville, Alabama,
Photo: Steve Cassidy
Huntsville, Alabama

Everyone loves clowns, so most cake decorators will be called upon to make one sooner or later. Dathern has hand-sculptured this artistic clown out of gum paste. He is placed on top of a white chocolate cupcake.

Design & photo: Carol Webb
Albany, Oregon

The animals were formed using the pictured mold, ELI #748 available from elegantlacemolds.com. Carol mixed the fondant to match the animals. She inserted white tusks in the elephant mold before adding the grey for the body. The lions mane was inserted first then the black ear and eyes. Paint the details according to the animal. Use a grass tip for the background area. The trees were made from pretzels topped with leaves using mold ELI #749.

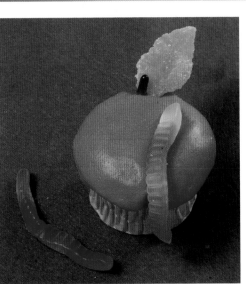

Design: Alexandria Pappas
Nashville, Tennessee

What could be a better way to start the school year than with this luscious apple for the teacher. The jumbo cupcake is frosted perfectly smooth with red frosting with a slight indentation at the stem and bottom end. A candy stem is inserted with a green gum drop leaf. A piece of spaghetti inserted into the leaf will hold it securely at the location of your choice into the apple. A green gummy worm accents the special treat.

Design: Irene Leach
Miami, Florida

The adorable little hand molded angel is admiring the tiny fish as they appear to be swimming around the sides of the fondant covered cake.

Design: Irene Leach
Miami, Florida

A hand molded toy train chugs atop a fondant cupcake and the base is surrounded with a fondant ribbon embossed with an impression roller from Cuqui's Designs.

October is such a fun time of the year with beautiful fall leaves, jack-o-lanterns and the fun characters of Halloween including black cats and spooky spiders.

Itsy Bitsy Spider

Supplies
- 1 large muffin
- 1 standard size gum ball
- Several pieces of spaghetti
- Fondant, walnut size black, pea size orange and white
- Orange frosting – either butter cream or fondant

Frosted muffin with indention

Cover gum ball with fondant

Place spider body on muffin

Frost the muffin with bright orange. Press an indentation in the top to hold the spider body. Roll a smooth ball of black fondant and place it in the palm of your hand. Firmly press a standard-size gum ball into the fondant. Completely cover the gum ball and roll it until smooth. For the eyes, flatten and elongate tiny balls of orange fondant and stick them to the face of the ball. Attach a tiny black dot to each eye for the pupil and highlight with a speck of white. You can also add an orange mouth and white teeth.

Adding eyes

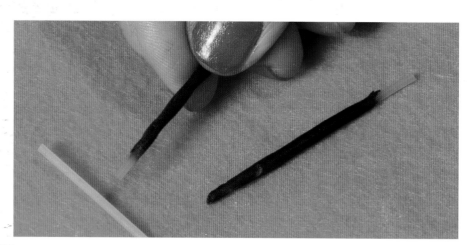

Cover spaghetti legs with black fondant

Arrange spider legs

Break the spaghetti into sixteen 2 inch long pieces. Roll each and cover with black fondant. Stick one end at the base of the spider body. Press another piece into the outer edge of the muffin and prop the two pieces together at the point. Press the two pieces together to secure the fondant. This forms one leg. Repeat this process for seven additional legs.

Fall Leaves

Supplies
- Small balls of fondant - brown, orange, red, green, yellow
- Leaf cookie cutter
- Flower former
- Paint brush
- Copper dusting powder
- candies

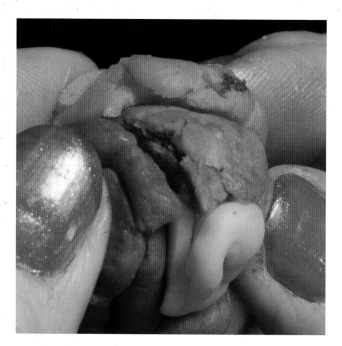

Blend several colors into a ball

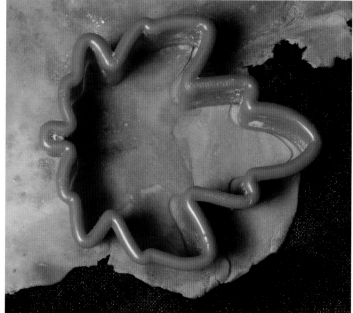

Cut leaves with a cookie cutter

Select small balls of several colors of fondant and press them together. Do not blend the colors too much or they will become one color rather than marbleized. Roll the ball to a thin sheet and cut with various size cookie cutters. It is best to roll small pieces at one time in order to keep the colors fresh. To achieve different realistic shapes, lay some inside the former and some molded over the outside.

Thin the leaf edges, vein with a dull table knife or veiner and place each in a flower former to dry. After the leaves are dry, brush them lightly with dry dusting color, either copper, bronze or gold tone to blend the leaf shades.

To form acorns, select a tan piece of candy such as "Milkfuls." Roll a marble size ball of brown fondant and place it on top of the candy to form a cap. Pinch and roll a tiny stem. Use the dull end of a paint brush handle to poke little indentations all over the cap.

Add veins and brush with luster powder

Form acorns

Make indentations in acorn cap

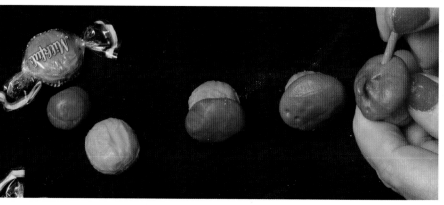

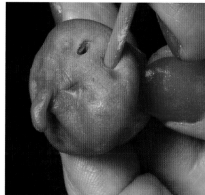

Supplies
- 2 dozen mini cupcakes
- Orange butter cream
- green butter cream
- Cake board or foam core board
- Small ball of black fondant

Arrange cup cakes on pumpkin shape board

Frost pumpkin shape

Arrange eyes and nose

97

Cut a pumpkin shape from a cake board or foam core board using the included pattern. Frost the board orange and arrange mini cupcakes to cover the entire board and stem, leaving the papers intact.

Generously apply orange butter cream to the top of the cupcake arrangement and frost the stem green. Let the frosting air dry slightly and smooth the top with a paper towel. Use the side of your hand to impress creases into the pumpkin to divide it into sections. Roll the ball of black fondant until it is thin and cut three triangles and a crescent shape. Place the triangles for the nose and eyes and place the crescent for the mouth.

Black Cat

Supplies
- 2 Standard cupcakes
- 1 sucker
- 1 mini cupcake
- Serrated knife
- Orange frosting
- Black fondant and tiny piece green fondant
- Small piece spaghetti

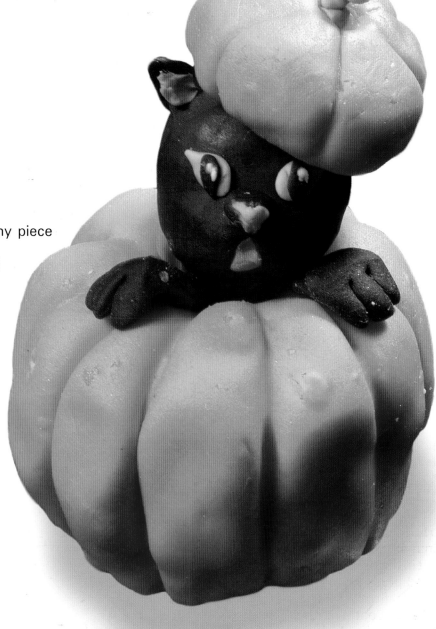

Remove the papers from two standard cupcakes. Frost between the two and cover them with butter cream or fondant. Cover them with orange and make vertical indentations around the pumpkin.

Stack cup cakes

Frost cup cakes

Cut mini cup cake in half

To form the cap of the pumpkin, remove the paper from one mini cupcake and cut it in half with a serrated knife. Frost one half with orange and make indentations (disregard the second half). Press a small ball of green fondant on a small piece of spaghetti leaving enough exposed to insert into the pumpkin lid.

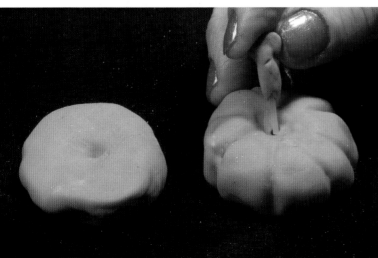

Pumpkin lid

To form the head, place a walnut-size ball of black fondant in the palm of your hand and press the ball of the sucker firmly into it. Work the fondant over the sucker to form the black cat head. Shape the nose area and pull up two pointed ears. Form slanted green eyes, black pupils, pink nose, pink ears, red tongue and secure them with a little water. Cut approximately 1-1/2 inch from the length of the sucker stick and insert it into the center of the pumpkin. Secure the pumpkin top with a little frosting. Form two little black paws and attach them at the base of the head.

Forming cats head

Insert head in pumpkin

Design, mold & photo: Carol Webb
  Albany, Oregon

Create a pattern for the sides of the little cake by laying the fondant on a mold and rolling from the center to each end. The fluffy bow is made from twenty-seven 2 inch long loops, dried then arranged to form the crowning touch to this lovely little cupcake. The mold is available from elegantlacemolds.com.

Design: Susan Zugehoer
Hebron, Kentucky

Marzipan cut outs of ghosts and bats placed on butter cream covered cupcakes provide quick to make treats.

Design: Anna Johnson
Louisville, Kentucky

This unique little bag is formed by placing a frosted cupcake, without the paper, in the center of a fruit roll up sheet and gathering the candy to the top of the cupcake. These would make perfect treats for the goblins at Halloween.

Design & photo: Kelly Lance
Gaston, Oregon

The scarecrow, birds and pumpkins are hand molded of gum paste. They could easily be formed from candy clay if they are to be eaten. The fondant covered cupcake is hidden inside the sheaf of cornstalks which were also made from rolled fondant. All pieces are accented with either paste or powdered colors mixed with lemon extract.

November
A Time for Thanks

Gobble Gobble

Supplies
- 1 standard size cupcake
- Fondant light brown and white
- Food writer pen
- Round cutters
- Dusting Powders

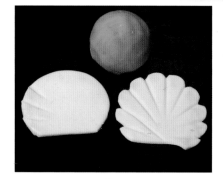

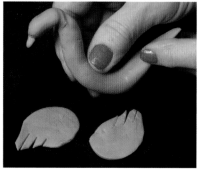

Frost cup cake body & make tail feathers

Form neck and wings

Paint eye

Remove paper and frost the entire cupcake in brown butter cream or fondant. Smooth the frosting for the body of the turkey. Shape a log of fondant for the neck and let it dry.

Cut a large round circle for the tail. Cut off the lower edge so it will sit flat. Mark the tail feathers and set aside to dry. Paint the dried feathers bright colors with dusting powder and attach to the back of the turkey with frosting.

Cut the wings, dry and attach them. Add the eyes with the food safe pen and attach the neck to the body with frosting.

Chocolate Delights

Supplies

- Thirteen 2 x 2 x2 inches cake squares
- Boards 4 x 4 inches, 6 1/2 x 6 1/2 inches, 9 x 9 inches
- One gum ball
- Candy corn
- Brown and Orange satin ribbon
- Piece brown fondant and orange fondant
- Thirteen acetate strips 2 x 8 inches
- Orange and Chocolate candy melts
- #18 star tip

Bake thirteen 2 x 2 x 2 inch cake squares. Frost the sides of seven squares with orange butter cream. Frost the top of these seven with chocolate. Frost the sides of the remaining six chocolate and the tops orange.

Cut a strip of clear acetate, 2 x 8 inches, and lay it on a piece of waxed paper. Melt orange candy melts and spread over the acetate. Lift the strip and wrap around the sides of an orange frosted cake. Allow the strip to remain on the cupcake until the candy is set. Gently remove the acetate from the cupcake leaving a slick, shiny surface. Repeat the process for the remaining squares, orange on orange and chocolate on chocolate.

Mold the turkey by covering a gum ball with brown fondant. Glue a semi-circle of candy corn to the back of the turkey bottom. Lay it flat to dry. Mold an orange fondant neck, allow it to dry, then secure it to the ball with frosting. Pipe butter cream borders around the top edge of each cupcake and stand candy corn around the base for the lower borders.

Frost cup cakes and add candy corn borders

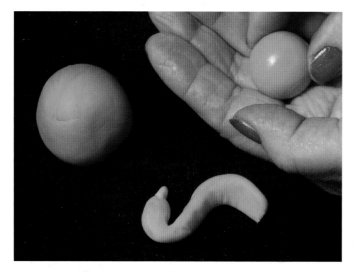

Cover turkey body with brown fondant

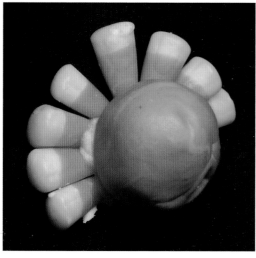

Candy corn tail feathers

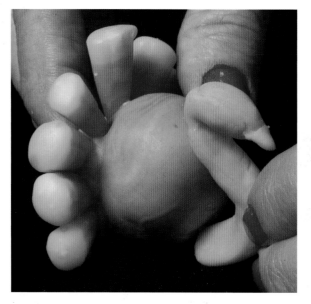

Add fondant neck

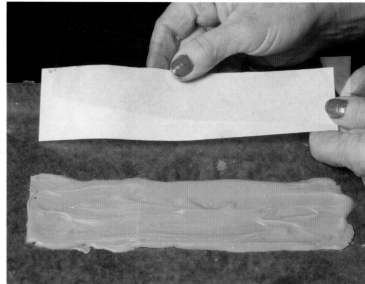

Spread chocolate on acetate strip

Wrap frosted acetate around cake

Remove acetate

Honeymoon Cottage

Supplies

- 2 small cakes baked in a mixing bowl
- Orange frosting, Brown frosting
- Fondant, orange, green, gray, black, white, brown
- Ivy cutter

Bake 2 small cakes

Bake two small cakes using a Pyrex baking dish, aluminum mixing bowl, or a two piece ball pan. Frost the two pieces together. Carve vertical groves with a serrated knife. Generously frost the pumpkin with orange butter cream. Smooth the cake with a paper towel, indenting the grooves. Cut tiny green ivy leaves and glue them up the grooves. Attach a brown stem, add windows and a door.

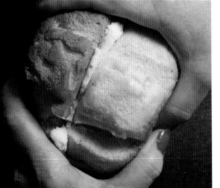

Frost cakes together

Frost pumpkin

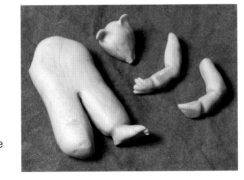

Steps to form mice

Form the mice from gray fondant. Mold the groom as pictured, form a log for the body. Divide the lower half for the legs and mold the feet. Form a tear drop shape head and two arms. The girl has a cone shape lower body. Dress the figures appropriately and place them by the cottage.

Ballerina Bear

Supplies

- 1 large muffin
- Pink frosting
- Pink sugar
- Edible glitter
- Fondant, pink, green, white

Frost and glitter cup cake

Cut bear skirt

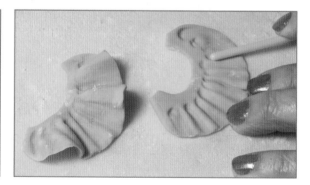

Ruffle skirt

Mold a little white fondant bear in a First Impression mold. Re-shape the arms and legs into ballerina position. Insert a skewer thru the standing leg and into the body. Set the bear aside to thoroughly dry.

Cut circles of pink, green, and white fondant. Place each on a cel pad and roll pleats with the smooth end of a small paint brush. Layer the colors and prop with small pieces of tissue to hold the ruffling while they dry. Add ballerina slippers and hair bows.

Frost a large muffin with pink frosting. Sprinkle it generously with pink sugar and glitter. Position the ballerina on the cupcake by inserting the skewer into the cupcake.

Insert skewer through the leg and into cupcake

Design: Vera Gooch
  Kings Mountain, Kentucky

  The understated beauty of the delicate string work on this white fondant covered treat is extraordinary. The extension work is accomplished with # 0 and royal frosting.

Design: Darlene Nold
Louisville, Kentucky

This old coon dog is sleeping on the porch during the heat of the day. This sleepy little fellow is molded in a mold from Sweet Express. Sugar rocks form the steps for the porch.

Opposite Page:
Design & photo: Earlene Moore
Lubbock, Texas

Earlene is well known for her realistic shotgun shells and turkey feathers so I feel very honored that she has willing shared her technique with us. The original wafer paper feathers were developed by Shirley Manbeck, also from Texas.

Make a feather veining mold from Sculpy, following directions on the package. Cut a wafer paper feather shape and place on the mold. Spray the feather with vodka, gently pressing into the veins. Place a skewer/toothpick on the center vein and place another feather shape on top of the skewer. Spray again with vodka and gently press to mold the two pieces together. Let the feather dry thoroughly before removing. Finish the coloring using non-toxic markers, food color pens or air brush coloring.

Mix Silicone Plastique and apply a thin layer to the detail of the top and bottom of a shotgun shell, then immediately apply a heavier layer over that. Allow the molds to sit untouched for approximately 2 hours for the silicone to set up. Cut out circles for the top/bottom with an Ateco tip 809 from gumpaste rolled to a thickness of 2 or 3 with a pasta machine. Press the gumpaste circles into the molds to the top and bottoms of the shotgun shells. Chill and remove the base piece from the molds and place on waxed paper until dry.

Make a pattern 2 x 2-1/4 inches for the circumference of the 12 gauge shotgun shells. Mark the straight line going around the shell with an angled spatula. Roll a 1/2 inch diameter threaded rod over the paste from the line down, to mark the tiny lines over the paste. Lay the pattern on the gumpaste and cut away the excess then wrap around a dowel rod over waxed paper. Paint the grooved and top section of the sugar shotgun shells with a mixture of vodka and strong red food coloring, thinned with piping gel. Let dry completely. Attach the disc to the hollow shell with royal icing. Paint the bottom section with a mixture of highlighter gold or silver dusting powder and lemon extract.

Design: Claudette Tidwell
Nashville, Tennessee

Great for Thanksgiving or even Halloween, this marzipan pumpkin is surrounded by miniature marzipan fall leaves.

Design: Claudette Tidwell
Nashville, Tennessee

Miniature marzipan replicas of delicious looking food adorns the tops of these butter cream covered cupcakes. Perfect treats for Thanksgiving.

Christmas Accents

Supplies
- 1 gum ball for each figure
- 1 standard cupcake
- Fondant – flesh for face and hands, black for boots, red or green
- 1 pointed ice cream cone
- #14 star tip and decorator bag
- Frostings – green or white
- Candies for the tree

The elf is formed by molding green fondant or gum paste over a standard size gum ball. They can be formed in different positions but this one is extremely tired from all the work. The arms, legs and hat are formed free hand with the green paste and completed with a small ball for the head. The same gum balls can be used to form Mr. or Mrs. Claus.

Santa's Tired Elf

The tree is piped with green royal and a leaf tip. Start at the base and pipe rows of leaves up and around the tree until you reach the top. Stick tiny colorful candies in the wet frosting.

To form the fluffy red bows, cut tiny strips of red fondant. Drape them over a small dowel and secure by pinching together. Let the loops dry over night then remove and arrange them to form a bow.

Steps to form tree

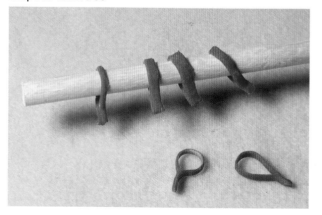

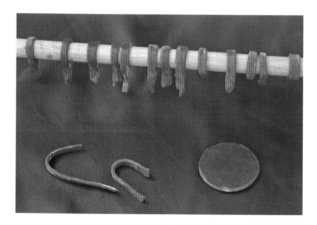

Form ribbon loops

Arrange loops to form bows

Red Nosed Reindeer

Supplies
- 1 standard cupcake
- 1 mini cupcake
- Brown frosting
- Small piece of foam core board
    - 2 curved pretzels
        - 1 maraschino cherry and a small piece of spaghetti
        - Fondant – pea size pieces of white and black

Place on foam core board

Cover head with brown frosting

Cut a piece of foam core board, using the included pattern. Remove the papers and cover 1 standard and 1 mini cupcake. Set them on the foam core board and completely cover them in brown frosting.

Position the 2 pretzels for deer antlers and secure them with a little frosting. Insert a small piece of spaghetti into the cherry and insert it for the nose. Roll tiny balls of white fondant for the eyes and press them into small ovals. Form smaller black ovals for the pupils and place them on the white. Attach the eyes onto the face of the deer.

Ho Ho Ho

Supplies
- 2 dozen mini cupcakes
- Butter cream frosting in pink, white and red
- Foam core board
- Fondant –pea size piece of black and white
- # 21 decorator tip and decorator bag

Arrange cup cakes on board

Frosted face

Add facial features

Cut a Santa head from foam core board using the pattern in this book. Cover the board with frosting and arrange mini cupcakes to cover the head, leaving the papers intact. Generously spread pink frosting on the center area of the top of the cupcakes and smooth. Frost the top area for the hat with red butter cream.

Place white butter cream and a #21 star tip into a decorating bag. Pipe the frosting in a swirling motion to form a curly beard and a furry hat. Roll out a small piece of black fondant and cut eyes. Place a ball of pink fondant for the nose.

Grandma's Holiday Treats

A favorite memory of Christmas is my grandmother's famous jam cake. Although she was not a decorator, she always meticulously placed walnut halves and colored gum drops on top of her creations. These cupcakes are the speedy, modern rendition of Grandma's cake.

Supplies
- Red/green gum drops
- Walnut halves
- Carmel frosting
- 1 spice cake mix
- 1-1/2 cups jam – any variety

Mix a spice cake mix according to the directions and add 1-1/2 cup jam. Bake the mixture in cupcake papers. Mix caramel icing by the following receipt and spread on top of the cupcakes. Alternate walnut halves, red or green gum drops on top of each cupcake.

Caramel Frosting
- 1 cup butter
- 1 pound brown sugar
- 1/2 cup cream
- 1 pound powdered sugar

Melt the butter and brown sugar and cook over a low heat. Stir constantly for two minutes. Add the cream and bring it to a boil. Remove from the heat and add 1 pound of sifter powdered sugar, mixing with a wisp. If it seems too thin add a little more sugar.

Garnish with gum drops and walnuts

Design: Alexandra Pappas
Nashville, Tennessee

Six mini cupcakes are grouped together to form a perfect little Christmas tree. Tiny candies and jelly beans create decorations for the tree. The trunk is a double width of brown liquorish twist and the little gifts are decorated sugar cubes.

Design: Susan Zugehoer
Hebron, Kentucky

A perfect little wreath is created by piping a circle of green around the top edge of the cupcake with a small writing tip or even a grass tip. The bow and decorations are piped on with a 1 or 2 tip and red frosting.

Design: Susan Zugehoer
Hebron, Kentucky

Each of these colorful designs is achieved by laying a stencil on the cupcake and covering with contrasting frosting or colored sugar. Gently lift the stencil to reveal a perfect design.

Design: Irene Leach
   Miami, Florida

This whimsical little snowman frolics above an impressed border of additional snowmen. The figure could be hand molded of fondant balls or you could cover a standard gum ball with white fondant for the body. Tiny red and blue accents form the hat and scarf.

Design, mold, & photo: Norm Davis & Zane Beg
   Annedale, Virginia

These beautiful angels could be adapted as Christmas angels, cupids for Valentine's Day or just a special occasion. Molds were skillfully created by Norm and Zane then molded in chocolate. The coloring brings the figurines to life. The beautiful leaves and flowers are formed in gum paste.

Design & photo: Vicky Harlan
Abbeville, South Carolina

To reproduce the package cupcake, cut red fondant in 1/4 inch strips, form and dry bow loops. When the loops are dry, cut and use two strips to create package "straps." Pipe butter cream the same color as the bow and add the loops to the center. Spray the completed bow with pearl dust.

To form the Christmas candle cupcakes, pipe pine boughs with grass tip #233 and green butter cream frosting. Wrap thin pretzels with red fondant and insert into the cupcake at various levels. Complete the design by piping yellow butter cream flames.

The wreath is formed using grass tip #233 to pipe 3 rows of "pine needles" around the top edge of the iced cupcake. Use a Jem small bow cutter to make a bow out of fondant and let dry. Add the bow and gold dragees to decorate. Spray with pearl dust.

Design: Claudette Tidwell
Nashville, Tennessee

Marzipan holly leaves cut with a gum paste cutter and berries are placed on a butter cream cupcake for a holiday treat.

Forming the arms and bodice

Impressed fondant covers a cupcake to form the bassinet

Design & photo: Carol Webb
Albany, Oregon

These doll cupcakes are made from regular size single cupcakes. To make the head, use a 1 inch gumball. Cover the gumball with a ball of flesh colored fondant. Cut the end of a straw in half, removing one side of the straw to form a half circle. Turn the end of the straw up to form a "U". This will imprint the mouth and sleepy eyes in the head. Take a tiny bit of flesh colored fondant to form the nose.

To form the bodice and arms of the doll above, use fondant in a ELI mold #526 and trim into a 4 inch circle. Form a 4 inch strip of flesh-colored fondant to make the arms. Lay a 1 inch sucker. over the arms and push it into them. The fold the fondant circle over the sucker and arms.

The same ELI mold is used to make the bottom of the dress. Trim the edges and place the fondant over the butter cream covered cupcake to form the skirt. Insert the sucker stick of the bodice into the center of the cupcake skirt. Glue the head on top of the body of the doll. Fold the hands together. The braided hair is formed with 3 strands of colored fondant braided.

The baby and bassinet is made in a similar way, using impressed fondant over a cupcake to form the bassinet.

Design: Diane Shavkin
Fishkill, New York

An impression rolling pin was rolled over the top of a fondant covered cake and a foam stamp pressed into the top to form the poinsettia. Holes were made with a sharp, pointed tool such as a toothpick. A small ruffle trims the base.

The second design is formed with an impression roller. A molded rose adorns the top and a fondant ruffle surrounds the base.

Design: Leigh Sipe
Harrodsburg, Kentucky

Tiny molded chocolate baby shoes brushed with pearl luster top this individual cake baked using a coffee filter in a 5 inch cake pan. The cake is frosted with butter cream. Tiny molded alphabet blocks, made in a First Impression mold, surround the base. The matching plate has baby ribbon inserted through the holes.

Design: Gail Forrester
Lenoir City, Tennessee

The Christmas tea pot set is formed from 3 jumbo, 1 regular and 1 mini cupcake. Invert 1 jumbo cupcake and ice the small end. Position an inverted regular cupcake on top of the iced end and invert the mini on top. Frost the sides of the stacked cupcakes and add a Hershey kiss shaped mound of butter cream to the top of the mini.

Using a 4-1/2 inch fluted cookie cutter cut several discs from the white fondant cutting out the center with a 2 inch round cookie cutter. Make a small pleat about every 1-1/4 inch. Attach the pre-formed and dried spout. Starting at the bottom of the tree, attach the fluted ring using a little

butter cream and continuing around with another ring until you reach the starting point. Repeat the same process for each ruffle continuing up the tree. When you reach the top, do not cut out the center of the fluted disc but drape over the top of the tree. Attach the handle with icing.

Trim the sides to make a square of each of the remaining jumbo cupcakes for the cream and sugar. Attach pre-formed candy cane handles and fill the sugar bowl with mini sugar cubes. Trim the tree with white fondant jewel dusted with snow sparkle and 1/8 inch round red jewels. Cut a star and attach for the lid handle.

Design & photo: Linda Mashni
Lexington, Kentucky

These adorable sleeping babies with diapers were made with a Sunflower Sugar Art mold (SM-043 baby with diaper). The babies facing up were made with a Holly Products mold. It has three sizes of heads on one mold and these were made with the middle size. The little hands are also made with a Holly Products mold. These molds were purchased through Global Sugar Art. The bassinets were made using the new Wilton rubber cupcake holders because Linda wanted it to match the top of the bassinet which was made of 50/50 fondant and gum paste molded in an egg shaped Wilton pan. The blankets were made using different rollers and imprinters.

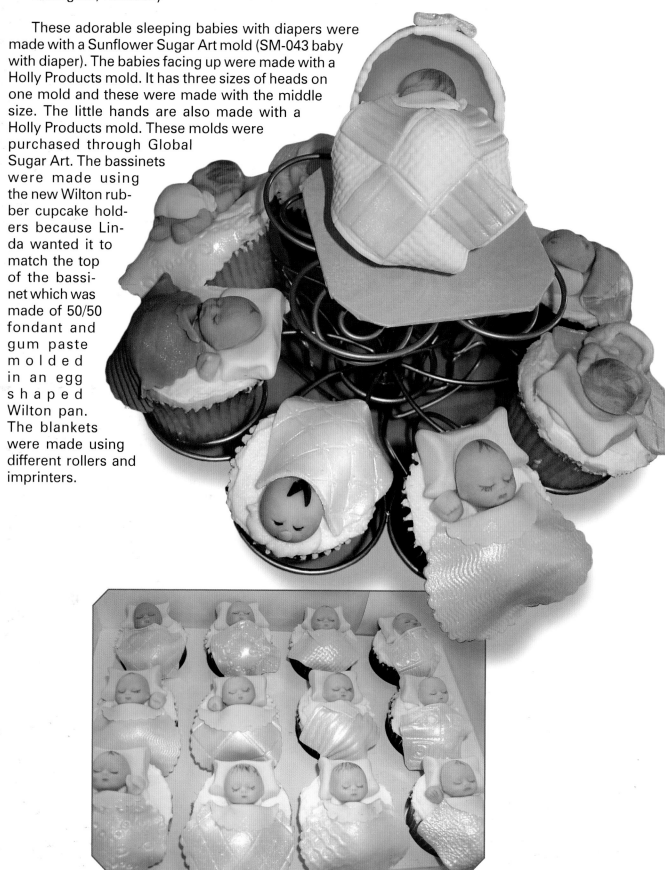

122

Design & photo: Norman Davis & Zane Begs
Annedale, Virginia

This creative and beautiful coral reef scene is a perfect retreat from the holiday and winter blues. Food Network Cake Challenge contestants Norm Davis and Zane Beg have created a beautiful underwater cupcake garden with confectionary flowers, colorful molded fish swimming by and gorgeous coral sprays.

Patterns *

**Chapter 8:
Gone Fishing**

**Chapter 5:
Derby Winner**

**Chapter 7:
Celebrate the Flag**

**Chapter 4:
Easter Bunny**

*NOTE: All patterns are shown 75% of original size. For full-sized patterns please enlarge 133%

Chapter 10:
Jack-O-Lantern

Chapter 11:
Gobble Gobble

Chapter 12:
Ho Ho Ho

Chapter 12:
Red Nosed
Reindeer

*NOTE: All patterns are shown 75% of original size. For full-sized patterns please enlarge 133%

Suppliers

AmeriColor
341 C. Melrose Street
Placentia, CA 92870

Marithe de Alvarado
Avenue Cuauhtemoc 950
Col. Narvarte
03020 Mexico, D.F.
011-525-523-7493

Bakery Craft
P.O. Box 37
West Chester, OH 45071
1-800-543-1673
www.bakerycrafts.com

CK Products
310 Racquet Drive
Fort Wayne, IN 46825
219-484-2517
www.ckproducts.com

Conways Confections
Darlene Nold
12220 Shelbyville Road
Louisville, KY 40243
502-245-1010
www.conwaysconfections.com

Cracker Barrel Old Country Store
www.crackerbarrel.com

Dec-O-Pac
3500 Thurston Ave.
Anoka, NM 55303

Fancy Flours
www.fancyflours.com

First Impressions Molds, LLC.
www.firstimpressionsmolds.com

Sweet Inspirations
Division of Cal-Java
19519 Business Center Drive
Northridge, CA 91324
www.caljavaonline.com

It's Personal
Bannon Crossing
Nicholasville, KY
589-245-GIFT

Make Your Own Molds - Plastique
1948 W. 8th Street
Cincinnati, OH 45204
513-244-2999
questions@makeyourownmolds.com

Nicholas Lodge
The International Sugar Art Collection
6060 McDonough Drive
Norcross GA 0093 1230
800-662-8925
nicklodge1@aol.com

Rosa's Designs - Rosa Viacava de Ortega
Lima Peru
www.rosasdesign.com

Beth Parvu Sugarpaste, LLC
538 East Ewing Avenue
South Bend, IN 46613
574-233-6525
www.sugarpaste.com

Geraldine Randlesome Creative Cutters
561 Edward Ave. Unit 2
Richmond Hill, Ontario
Canada L4C9W6
888-805-3444
www.creativecutters.com

Miguel Roque
Lima, Peru

Kathy Scott Sweet Express
P.O. Box 218
Abbeville, SC 29620-0218
www.sweetexpress.com

Linda Shonk Sweet Art Inc.
6011 E. Hanna Avenue Suite E
Indianapolis, IN 46203
317-787-3647
www.choco-pan.com

PME Sugarcraft Tools
Distributed by CK Products
Fort Wayne, IN 46824
mail@ckproducts.com

Carol Webb The Cakery
2118 Meadow Place SE
Albany, OR 97321-5560
www.elegantlacemolds.com

Wilton Industries
2240 W. 75th Street
Woodbridge, IL 60571
888-824-9520
www.wilton.com

Acknowledgments

Contributing Cupcake Decorators

Mirta Carvajal De Alvarado
Av. San Felipe 1120-202
Lima 11, Peru
511-571-3404

Mary Ball Burton
9813 Johnson Street
Crown Point, IN 46307-2425

Zane Beg – The Sweet Life
4950 Sunset Lane
Annandale, VA
703-750-3266
www.thesweetlife.com

Bonnie Blackburn
P.O. Box 6
Feversham, Ont. Canada, NOCICO
519-922-2713

Steve Cassidy Photography
2614 Artie Street suite #28
Huntsville, AL 35805
286-536-4604

Christine Clark
12026 Diamondview Dr.
Cincinnati, OH 45241
515-563-1178

Diane Constant
2311 Zhale Smite Road
LaGrange, KY 40031
502-222-8763

Norm Davis – The Sweet Life
4950 Sunset Lane
Annandale, VA
703-750-3266
www.thesweetlife.com

Gail Forrester
Lenoir city, TN 37771
865-986-4154 / 865-986-9456

Falencia A. Frazier
3219 Dalmellington Ct.
Cincinnati, OH 45251
513-227-4183

Denise Gieske
6334 Tara Brooke Ct.
Hamilton, OH 45011
513-737-0937

Vera Gooch
P.O. Box 52
Kings Mountain, KY 40442
606-365-7756

Wendy Hack
804 McKinley Avenue
Louisville, KY 40217
502-637-1584

Vicky Harlen
528 Highway 20
Abbeville, SC 29620
864-446-7838

Robert Holsinger
4793 Keith Circle
Colorado Springs, CO 80916
719-321-8242

Brenda Hoye
4758 U.S. Highway 40
West Jefferson, OH 43162

Jacque Hutsen – Daisy Lane Cakes
4192 Wood Knoll Dr.
Batavia, OH 45103
513-753-5208

Kelly Lance - Artful Decadence
10118 SW High Lane
Gaston, OR 97119
503-985-3133

Anna Johnson
12527 Davis Court
Louisville, KY 40243
502-290-5120

Linda Mashni - Classic Cakes by Linda
2265 Abbeywood Road
Lexington, KY 40515
859 489 8392

Dathern Moon - Elegant Wedding Cakes
1502 Cheermont Drive SE
Huntsville, AL 35801-2108
256-536-2629 / 256-539-3794

Earlene Moore - Earlene's Cakes
1323 E. 78th Street
Lubbock, TX 79404
806-745-2230

Cecilia Morana - Cecilia Morana's School
Maria Fernanda Morana Photographs
Jirrey Avenue 3002
Capital Federal 1426 Argentina
011-541-4554-7312
www.cecilia-morana.ar

Sue Nelson
8657 Susanview Lane
Cincinnati, OH 45244
513-474-6859

Darlene Nold – Conways Cakes and Candies
12220 Shelbyville Road
Louisville, KY 40243
502-245-1010

Rosa Viacava de Ortega–CEO
GNE El Atelier del Azucar
Av. Brasil 1141
Lima, Peru, Lima 11
511-423-4210

Alexandra Pappas
3933 Eckhart Drive
Nashville, TN 37211
615-834-5944

Elizabeth Parvu - Sugar Paste /
Crystal Colors
538 E. Ewing Av.
South Bend, IN 46613
574-233-6524
www.sugarpaste.com

Lou Putnam – Photography
South Bend, IN 46613

Maria Regina Padel Rodrigues
Ave. Atlantica 554/402
Rio De Janeiro, Brazil 22010-000
55-212-542-3916

Kathy Scott – Sweet Expressions
PO Box 218
Abbeville, SC 29620
864-446-3137

Diane Shavkin – The Magic Touch
32 Hampshire Road
Fishkill, NY 12524
845-897-9562

Leigh H. Sipe – Cakes By Leigh
551 Brewers Mill Road
Harrodsburg, KY 40330
859-366-4368

Steven Stellingwerf
2915 Lymegrass Ave.
Sioux Falls, SD 57107
605-339-8317

Angie Thacker
210 Green Avenue
Groveport, OH, 43125
614-580-3823

Claudette B. Tidwell
7544 Lakeview Drive
Nashville, TN 37209
615-356-3746

Leasa Shake Tucker
4014 S. 1st. Street
Louisville, KY 40214
502-361-5850

Mariella Ortega Viacava
2040 NW 89 Ave.
Pembroke Pines, FL 33024
954-885-8770

Carol Webb
Elegant Lace Mold by The Cakery
2118 SE Meadow PL
Albany, OR 97322
541-926-0025

Susan Zugehoer
1791 Conway Hills Drive
Hebron, KY 41048
589-586-5683